# DEVELOPING MATHEMATICS

**Customisable teaching resources for mathematics**

# UNDERSTANDING SHAPES AND MEASURES

## Ages 6–7

Hilary Koll and Steve Mills

D1079244

A & C Black • London

# Contents

## Understanding shape

Visualise common 2-D shapes and 3-D solids; identify shapes from pictures of them in different positions and orientations; sort, make and describe shapes, referring to their properties. Identify reflective symmetry in patterns and 2-D shapes and draw lines of symmetry in shapes

### Follow and give instructions involving position, direction and movement

### Recognise and use whole, half and quarter turns, both clockwise and anticlockwise; know that a right angle represents a quarter turn

## Measuring

Estimate, compare and measure lengths, weights and capacities, choosing and using standard units (m, cm, kg, litre) and suitable measuring instruments

CR
Sib
IS
UND

## Read the numbered divisions on a scale, and interpret the divisions between them, for example on a scale from 0 to 25 with intervals of 1 shown but only the divisions 0, 5, 10, 15 and 20 numbered; use a ruler to draw and measure lines to the nearest centimetre

## Use units of time (seconds, minutes, hours, days) and know the relationships between them; read the time to the quarter hour; Identify time intervals, including those that cross the hour

Published 2008 by A & C Black Publishers Limited
36 Soho Square, London W1D 3QY
www.acblack.com

ISBN 978-1-4081-0058-5

Copyright text © Hilary Koll and Steve Mills 2008
Copyright illustrations © Gaynor Berry 2008
Copyright cover illustration © Jan McCafferty 2008
Editors: Lynne Williamson and Marie Lister
Designed by Billin Design Solutions Ltd

The authors and publishers would like to thank Catherine Yemm and Judith Wells for their advice in producing this series of books.

A CIP catalogue record for this book is available from the British Library.

Printed and bound in Great Britain by Halstan Printing Group, Amersham, Buckinghamshire.

A&C Black uses paper produced with elemental chlorine-free pulp, harvested from managed sustainable forests.

# Introduction

**100% New Developing Mathematics: Understanding Shapes and Measures** is a series of seven photocopiable activity books for children aged 4 to 11, designed to be used during the daily maths lesson. The books focus on the skills and concepts for Understanding Shapes and Measuring as outlined in the National Strategy's *Primary Framework for literacy and mathematics*. The activities are intended to be used in the time allocated to pupil activities; they aim to reinforce the knowledge and develop the facts, skills and understanding explored during the main part of the lesson and to provide practice and consolidation of the objectives contained in the Framework document.

## Understanding shape

The 'Understanding shape' strand of the *Primary Framework for mathematics* is concerned with helping pupils to develop awareness and understanding of the properties of shapes, special concepts and ideas of position and location. This strand includes the properties of 2-D and 3-D shapes, including angles and symmetries together with ways of describing positions in grids such as using co-ordinates.

## Measuring

The 'Measuring' strand of the *Primary Framework for mathematics* covers the main measurement topics such as length, mass and capacity, together with ideas of time, area and perimeter. These topics include estimating, comparing and measuring, including using standard metric units and converting between them.

## Understanding Shapes and Measures Ages 6–7

supports the teaching of mathematics by providing a series of activities to develop spatial vocabulary in order to increase awareness of properties of shape and measurement concepts. The following objectives are covered:

- visualise common 2-D shapes and 3-D solids; identify shapes from pictures of them in different positions and orientations; sort, make and describe shapes, referring to their properties;
- identify reflective symmetry in patterns and in 2-D shapes and draw lines of symmetry in shapes;
- follow and give instructions involving position, direction and movement;
- recognise and use whole, half and quarter turns, both clockwise and anticlockwise; know that a right angle represents a quarter turn;
- estimate, compare and measure lengths, weights and capacities choosing and using standard units (m, cm, kg, litre) and suitable measuring instruments;

- read the numbered divisions on a scale, and interpret the divisions between them (for example on a scale from 0 to 25 with intervals of 1 shown but only the divisions 0, 5, 10, 15 and 20 numbered); use a ruler to draw and measure lines to the nearest centimetre;
- use units of time (seconds, minutes, hours, days) and know the relationships between them; read the time to the quarter hour; identify time intervals, including those that cross the hour.

## Extension

Some of the activity sheets end with a challenge (**Now try this!**) which reinforces and extends the children's learning, and provides the teacher with an opportunity for assessment. These might include harder questions than those in the main part of the activity sheet. Some extension activities are open-ended questions and provide opportunity for the children to think mathematically for themselves. Occasionally the extension activity will require additional paper or for children to write on the reverse of the sheet itself. Many of the activities encourage the children to generate their own questions or puzzles for a partner to solve.

## Organisation

Very little equipment is needed, but it will be useful to have the following resources available: coloured pencils, counters, cubes, scissors, glue, squared paper, sticky shapes, dice, counters, small mirrors, 2-D shapes, solid shapes, rulers, string, metre sticks, paper for folding and cutting, scissors, weighing scales, gram and kilogram weights, variety of containers, 1-litre containers, dotty squared paper, small analogue clocks with moveable hands, and digital clocks.

Where possible, the children's work should be supported by ICT equipment, such as software on an interactive whiteboard, for rotating a picture using drawing tools in a word-processing package or using image-editing software. It is also vital that the children's experiences are introduced in real-life contexts and through practical activities. The teachers' notes at the foot of each page and the more detailed notes on pages 6 to 13 suggest ways in which this can be done effectively.

To help teachers select appropriate learning experiences for the children, the activities are grouped into sections within the book. However, the activities are not expected to be used in this order unless stated otherwise. The sheets are intended to support, rather than direct, the teacher's planning.

Some activities can be made easier or more challenging by masking or substituting numbers, for example in time activities. You may wish to re-use pages by copying them onto card and laminating them.

## Accompanying CD

The enclosed CD-ROM contains electronic versions of the activity sheets in the book for printing, editing, saving or display on an interactive whiteboard. This means that modifications can be made to differentiate the activities to suit individual pupils' needs. See page 14 for further details.

## Teachers' notes

Brief notes are provided at the foot of each page, giving ideas and suggestions for maximising the effectiveness of the activity sheets. These can be masked before copying.

Solutions and further explanations of the activities can be found on pages 6 to 13, together with examples of questions that you can ask.

## Whole-class warm-up activities

The tools provided in A & C Black's Maths Skills and Practice CD-ROMs can be used as introductory activities for use with the whole class. In the Maths Skills and Practice CD-ROM 2 (ISBN 9780713673180) the following activities and games could be used to introduce or reinforce 'Understanding Shapes and Measures' objectives:

- Boot camp
- Boot camp II
- Diggy dog
- Patterns
- Weight lab
- Volume lab
- Crazy clocks
- Symmetry

The following activities provide some practical ideas that can be used to introduce or reinforce the main teaching part of the lesson, or provide an interesting basis for discussion.

## Time moves on

In the same way that children sitting in a circle might say numbers in a sequence, for example 2, 4, 6, 8…, begin by saying a time, such as 4 o'clock. Moving around the circle, ask the children to say the time that is an hour later or earlier, for example 4 o'clock, 5 o'clock, 6 o'clock, 7 o'clock. Once the children understand the idea, time sequences that involve counting on or back in steps of

half an hour or one quarter of an hour can be continued, such as 7 o'clock, quarter past 7, half past 7, quarter to 8. Hold up a clock to show the times and discuss different ways of saying the same time, for example quarter past 7, 7

## Keep your head down

To help the children develop a sense of a minute, ask them to sit at their tables with their heads down in their arms. Say, 'starting from now' and ask them to keep their heads down until the point when they think one minute has passed. Encourage them to count very slowly to 60 to help them. At the point they think one minute is up they should quietly stand up and remain standing still and quiet to see when the others will decide a minute has passed. When a minute is reached do not announce it aloud, but hold up something to show those that are standing how long a minute is. Usually, at first, the children stand far too quickly but with practice they gain a more appropriate estimate. Children could practise this using a one-minute sand timer.

## Turn, turn, turn

Ask the children to stand facing the front of the classroom with their eyes closed. Call out instructions involving making quarter, half or whole turns clockwise or anti-clockwise. Encourage them to turn slowly and not to look at other children.

## Behind the wall

You will need a selection of paper shapes such as triangles, circles, rectangles, squares, etc. Using a piece of cardboard or a book as a screen, gradually slide one of the shapes behind the screen to reveal part of the shape over the top for the children to see. Ask: *What shape might this be? Could it be more than one shape? What is special about the angle at this corner? Can you tell me something else about the shape you think this is?* Gradually reveal more and more of the shape until it has been correctly identified. 3-D shapes could also be used for this activity.

# Notes on the activities

## Shapes and Measures

**Visualise common 2-D shapes and 3-D solids; identify shapes from pictures of them in different positions and orientations; sort, make and describe shapes, referring to their properties. Identify reflective symmetry in patterns and 2-D shapes and draw lines of symmetry in shapes**

It is vital that the children are given extensive opportunity to work practically with shapes, construction materials, boxes, containers, sand, water and so on, in order to develop a broad understanding of the nature and properties of 2-D and 3-D shapes. The following activities can supplement these practical tasks and provide contexts and stimuli that can be more fully explored in the classroom. Encourage the children to develop vocabulary skills by ensuring that activities are undertaken in pairs or small groups and that whole-class discussions take place frequently. The activities below can be used to encourage the children to develop language skills and to develop awareness of the properties of shapes.

### Spot the shapes (page 15)

As the children become more familiar with standard shapes they will begin to recognise them when several shapes overlap. This activity can be used as an assessment to see how visually perceptive the children are in distinguishing overlapping shapes. Encourage them to make their own designs, perhaps by drawing round shapes, and to ask a partner to say which shapes they used.

**SUGGESTED QUESTIONS:**

- What shapes can you see here?
- Can you draw one for me?
- How many sides/corners does this shape have?
- What is the name of this shape?
- How many sides does it have?

### Sticky labels (page 16)

At the start of the lesson revise the common shape names and their properties, recording the number of sides of pentagons, hexagons, triangles, rectangles, octagons and squares on the board.

**SOLUTIONS:**

| | | |
|---|---|---|
| £4.50 | £5.20 | |
| £3.00 | £4.30 | £4.30 |
| £4.50 | £3.80 | £5.20 |
| £3.90 | £3.90 | £4.50 |
| £3.90 | £3.00 | £4.80 |

**SUGGESTED QUESTIONS:**

- Are the sides of this shape curved or straight?
- How many sides/corners does this have?
- How many sides does an octagon have?

### True or false? (page 17)

This activity also addresses the objective 'Describing and locating regions in a grid' where children use letters to describe the column and numbers to describe the row, for example A4 or C2.

Watch out for those children who incorrectly answer 'false' to the first question as this suggests that they do not appreciate that 2-D and 3-D shapes can be in any position or orientation and will still be classed as the same shape.

**SOLUTIONS:**

| | |
|---|---|
| true | false |
| true | true |
| true | false |
| true | false |

**SUGGESTED QUESTIONS:**

- Do you know what this shape is called?
- Describe the shape to me. What does it remind you of?
- How many sides/corners has it?

### Open up: 1 and 2 (pages 18–19)

At the start of the lesson hold up a symmetrical shape, already folded along its mirror line and explain to the children that you have folded a shape in half to make this one. Ask them to imagine the shape being opened out and invite them to describe the whole shape to you, referring to the numbers of sides, angles and its general shape. Then unfold the shape and discuss it further. Provide the children with Open up: 1 and ask them to imagine these shapes being opened up. Once they have predicted the number of sides for each shape they can be given the solutions on Open up: 2. The children should cut out the full shapes and fold them along the dotted lines to check, before opening out and checking their predictions.

**SUGGESTED QUESTIONS:**

- Can you imagine this square being opened out?
- How many sides will the whole shape have?

### Flat shape speedway! (page 20)

For this game the children should work in pairs. Each pair will need a dice, a counter each and one sheet (ideally enlarged onto A3 paper). Small mirrors should also be provided so that the children can check lines of symmetry.

**SUGGESTED QUESTIONS:**

- Do you know the name of this shape?
- How many sides/right angles/lines of symmetry has this shape?

### Crazy colours (page 21)

Some children experience difficulty in identifying 3-D shapes from pictures of them. Before beginning the activity, discuss the shapes shown on the sheet and ask the children to select them from a set of real solid shapes. Discuss the 2-D shapes of the faces of the 3-D shapes and ensure the children know the meaning of the word 'face' in this context. Be aware of children who do not yet appreciate that 3-D shapes can be in any position or orientation and are still the same shape. Note that technically the cubes could be ticked red and also pink, since squares are types of rectangles. This could be discussed with more confident pupils if thought appropriate.

**SUGGESTED QUESTIONS:**

- What shapes are the faces of a cube/cuboid?
- Which shapes have one or more curved faces?

## Solids speedway! (page 22)

For this game, the children should work in pairs. Each pair will need a dice, a counter each, and one sheet (ideally enlarged onto A3 paper). Ensure that children are familiar with the term 'vertices' or alter the term before copying to 'corners' if more appropriate. Discuss shapes such as cylinders and spheres that have no vertices and ensure the children appreciate that faces can be curved or flat, for example a sphere has one curved face. The sheet could also be altered to include edges for variety. Provide 3-D shapes for examination.

**SUGGESTED QUESTIONS:**

- Do you know the name of this shape?
- How many faces/vertices has this shape?
- Are its faces curved or straight?

## Guess the shape (page 23)

It is important that the children have as much experience with actual solid shapes as possible. Children, in pairs, could be provided with the full set of shapes and asked to match up each card with the correct shape.

**SOLUTIONS:**

sphere
cube
square-based pyramid
cylinder

tetrahedron (or octohedron)
cone
cuboid (or cube)

**SUGGESTED QUESTIONS:**

- Look at the solid shapes. Which has only one curved face?
- How many edges has this cylinder?
- Can you find a matching card for this shape?

## Exercise pairs (page 24)

This activity is most suitably given after the children have had practical experience of trying to mirror the movements of a partner. It can help them to appreciate the nature of symmetry, encourage them to see it in real-life situations and help them to become familiar with symmetry vocabulary.

**SUGGESTED QUESTIONS:**

- Can you make a shape that is the reflection of your partner's body shape?
- Which two cards make a symmetrical pattern?
- Can you see that this is the shape that you would see if a mirror was placed next to the person?

## Mirror mania (page 25)

This activity can be introduced to the class using some birthday cards. Hold them next to a mirror and ask the children to look at the reflection and comment on what they see. Encourage them to notice that any pictures or letters on the card are reflected and so face the other way. Choose a simple design and draw the reflection, asking the children to say which colours go where in the reflection.

**SUGGESTED QUESTIONS:**

- Have you checked your reflection?
- Hold the mirror next to the card. Lift the mirror and check your colouring underneath.

## Snip, snip (page 26)

This activity involves lines of symmetry (fold lines) in different orientations, including where the lines are diagonal. All shapes have only one line of symmetry. Encourage the children to use a ruler for this activity and to use small mirrors to check their answers.

**SUGGESTED QUESTIONS:**

- Where do you think the fold line must be?
- Can you use the mirror to check?

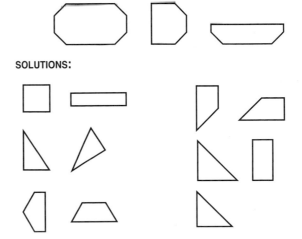

## Paper shapes (page 27)

This visualisation activity encourages the children to predict the shape when a piece of paper is folded in half. At the start of the lesson demonstrate folding a shape such as an octagon in half along different lines of symmetry, and counting the number of sides of the folded shape, for example:

**SOLUTIONS:**

**SUGGESTED QUESTIONS:**

- Can you fold this shape in another way?
- What about if you folded it lengthways?
- Can this shape be made if we folded this shape in half?

## Follow and give instructions involving position, direction and movement

Children should begin to develop an understanding of a range of positional, direction and distance words including those below. They should also be able to follow and give a set of instructions involving these words and be able to solve related problems.

*position, over, under, above, below, beneath, top, bottom, side, on, in, outside, inside, around, in front, behind, front, back, before, after, beside, next to, opposite, apart, between, up, down, forwards, backwards, sideways, across, close, far, near, along, through, to, from, towards, away from, movement, slide, roll, turn, stretch, bend*

### Pirate map (page 28)

This activity helps to develop using and applying skills such as trial and improvement, perseverance and visualisation. Children should cut out the cards and move them into position so that every statement is true.

**SOLUTIONS:**

| | | | |
|---|---|---|---|
| anchor | hut | parrot | tree |
| flag | cave | cannon | ship |
| chest | volcano | bridge | skull |

**SUGGESTED QUESTIONS:**

- Where is the cave?
- Is the parrot above or below the cannon?
- What is to the left of the bridge?
- What is under the anchor?

### School play (page 29)

This activity is enhanced if the children are introduced to it practically. Arrange some chairs in the hall and ask several children to sit in some positions. Ask other children to explain the position of those children and how they got there from a fixed point, for example the entrance. The sheet can be used as an assessment activity to see whether the children can follow simple sets of instructions involving direction and distance.

**SUGGESTED QUESTIONS/PROMPT:**

- Can you follow this set of instructions?
- Where would you end up?
- Remember to start at the entrance each time.

### In the kitchen (page 30)

This activity involves a range of positional vocabulary that children should use to describe the locations of a range of items.

For children who struggle to recall 'left' and 'right' invite them to hold out their hands, palms away from them as if telling someone to stop with both hands. By pulling their thumbs down only the left hand can make an L shape indicating left. The right produces a back-to-front L and therefore is not left, but right.

**SUGGESTED QUESTIONS:**

- Is the milk above or below the tissues?
- What is to the left of the tissues?
- What is under the shampoo?

### Avoid the zombies (page 31)

As children work in pairs to describe routes, they should be encouraged to record them accurately. There are different ways that the routes could be described, such as referring to turning and moving forwards or in relation to the whole grid, for example move up 1, then left 2, etc. Either approach is valid and the children could be encouraged to discuss which way of directing they find easier.

**SUGGESTED QUESTIONS:**

- Can you follow another group's instructions?
- Where would you end up?

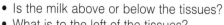

### The hamster run (page 32)

This sheet can be used as a stimulus for children making up their own escaped pet story. This could be linked to writing activities and the children could use the word-bank from this sheet to include in their story.

**SUGGESTED QUESTIONS:**

- Can you describe where the hamster went?
- Can anyone think of a better way of saying 'The hamster went along there…'?
- Which direction did the hamster go? Did it go under/over or between anything?

## Recognise and use whole, half and quarter turns, both clockwise and anticlockwise; know that a right angle represents a quarter turn

The basis of all angle work is the idea of turning. Many children have struggled with the ideas of angle because they have been given insufficient time to appreciate turn and moved too quickly on to static angles, causing misconceptions that the angle between two lines is related to line length, arc length, distance between the two end points of the lines etc. and not related to the amount of turn that would take one line onto the other.

Thus it is very important that children explore turns practically before they begin to explore them in static pictures. They should recognise and make whole, half and quarter turns as a precursor for understanding and recognising the nature of right angles.

### Rotating pictures (page 33)

This activity is best introduced using software on an interactive whiteboard, for example by rotating a picture using drawing tools in a word-processing package or by rotating using image editing software. By continuously clicking the rotate button (turning the picture through 90° each time) the children can see that four quarter turns return the picture to its original orientation.

**SUGGESTED QUESTIONS:**

- If we make two quarter turns is this the same as a half turn?
- The picture is the right way up. What will it look like after a half turn? How could we describe the picture now? (upside down)

## In a spin (page 34)

This activity should be introduced practically. Place a letter on each of the four walls of the classroom, for example A, D, R, E. Call out instructions like those on the sheet to spell words such as DARE, DEAR, READ, ARE, EAR, RED, etc. The activity sheet can then be used as an assessment to see which children can successfully follow instructions involving half and quarter turns both clockwise and anticlockwise. Remind the children of the directions of clockwise and anticlockwise.

As a further extension activity, the children could also be given their own letters, such as T, R, A, E and asked to write their own similar instructions to spell out simple words for others to solve, such as RATE, TEAR, TARE, ATE, EAR, TEA, RAT, ART, ARE, TAR, etc.

**SUGGESTED QUESTION:**

- What do you notice about making a half turn clockwise and making a half turn anticlockwise?

## Feeding time (page 35)

At the start of the lesson, show how the angles between scissor blades link turning with static angles. Demonstrate using a pair of scissors how the blades can be turned to create larger or smaller angles. Show a right angle and encourage children to identify when you are holding the blades at right angles to each other. This can be made into a game, where you keep moving the scissors and the children put their hands on their heads when it shows right angles. When the children play the game with the cards from the sheet, encourage them to think about scissor angles to help them compare the angles.

**SUGGESTED QUESTIONS:**

- A right angle is a quarter turn. True or false?
- Is this angle larger or smaller than a right angle?
- How can you check?

## Hexagon handiwork (page 36)

There are many different hexagons that can be drawn on a 4 by 4 dotted grid. Examples of hexagons that contain right angles include the following:

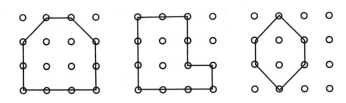

**SUGGESTED QUESTIONS:**

- How many sides does a hexagon have?
- Does this hexagon have any right angles?
- Can you mark them?

## Power-robots! (page 37)

This activity involves static pictures where the children must identify right angles. They should cut out and use the right-angle gobbler to check the angles.

**SOLUTIONS:**

 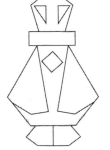

The left-hand robot has 18 right angles.
The right-hand robot has 15 right angles.

**SUGGESTED QUESTION:**

- If you twist the paper can you see whether there are any other right angles that you have missed?

## Estimate, compare and measure lengths, weights and capacities, choosing and using standard units (m, cm, kg, litre) and suitable measuring instruments

Initially, young children should begin to compare the relative sizes of objects and use a range of appropriate vocabulary. The next step is for them to begin to appreciate that lengths, weights and capacities can be described more accurately if compared with a uniform unit, for example when measuring weight the heaviness of each object could be described by the number of small cubes that it balances. This allows for many different objects to be compared without needing to compare them all directly. This idea of a uniform unit is the basis of measurement. Once children have had experience in measuring lengths with non-standard units such as footsteps, worms, cubes, etc. they can begin to be shown that people use 'standard' units of length, such as centimetres (for small lengths) and metres (for larger lengths). Similarly, the idea of cubes as a unit of weight begins to be replaced by grams and kilograms, and for capacity millilitres and litres eventually replace spoonfuls, cups and buckets. Children of this age are beginning to become familiar with centimetres, metres, grams, kilograms and litres.

## The metre beater game (page 38)

These cards can be used for a range of comparing activities, such as the following:

- Working in pairs, the children can pick a card each and say the difference between the two lengths.
- Cards can be placed face down. A target length can be chosen and the children pick a card each and see who has the length closer to the chosen target.
- More confident children can write the lengths in metres, in centimetres, or in both.

### SUGGESTED QUESTIONS:

- Do you think this is larger or smaller than one metre?
- Can you show me with your hands how long you think this length is?

## Going to great lengths (page 39)

Children need to appreciate when it is best to use centimetres (for measuring smaller lengths) and when it is best to use metres (for measuring longer lengths). Where the children give different answers from those below, discuss how long they think the item is and encourage them to estimate it in metres or centimetres.

Solutions:

| | |
|---|---|
| 1. metres | 2. centimetres |
| 3. centimetres | 4. metres |
| 5. centimetres | 6. centimetres |
| 7. metres | 8. metres |
| 9. centimetres | 10. metres |

### SUGGESTED QUESTION/PROMPT:

- About how wide do you think a butterfly is?
- Show me with your fingers. Now measure with a ruler to check your answer.

## Snail race (page 40)

This activity links with estimating positions on a number line whilst reinforcing an understanding of the relationship between centimetres and metres. It is best if this activity is introduced to the children visually, using six metre sticks or tables, each one metre long, and objects to represent the snails. Place the 'snail'

objects in various positions along the metre stick/table and ask the children to estimate how many centimetres along from the left it is. Also, ask how far each snail has to go to reach the end, to link with number pairs that total 100. Discuss fractions such as half a metre, quarter of a metre and so on and ask how many centimetres these are equivalent to.

### SUGGESTED QUESTIONS:

- How far do you think this snail has travelled?
- About how far has it left to go?

## Crunchy carrots (page 41)

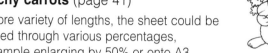

For more variety of lengths, the sheet could be enlarged through various percentages, for example enlarging by 50% or onto A3.

### SUGGESTED QUESTIONS:

- How many centimetres long do you think this carrot is?
- Can you explain to me how you estimated that?
- Which of these two do you think is longer?

## Doggy differences (page 42)

At the start of the lesson, discuss whether any children have dogs at home and if so what breed they are. Invite a child to describe how heavy their dog is, for example: 'Can you easily lift it up?' 'Is it too heavy to lift up?' Explain that we use kilograms to find out and compare how heavy things are. Pass round a kilogram weight and ask the children to say whether a dog is heavier or lighter than this. Discuss how heavy different breeds are and, where possible, find objects of an equivalent amount, such as: a bag of potatoes, a chair, a pile of books, etc.

### SUGGESTED QUESTIONS:

- How did you work out the difference between those two weights?
- Do you think that you weigh more or less than a chihuahua?

## Doggy dilemmas (page 43)

Demonstrate with a set of balance scales how things that balance remain horizontal when let go and things that do not balance tilt, with the heavier going down further. Explain that some of these pictures show things that will balance and others do not. The child's job is to find out which are which, using the information on the 'Doggy differences' cards.

### SUGGESTED QUESTIONS:

- Do these balance?
- How heavy are the things in the left-hand pan?
- How heavy are the things in the right-hand pan?
- Are they equal? So will they balance?

## Marble mania (page 44)

Children should be given practical experience of weighing marbles and jars to reinforce this activity. Once the weights of objects are known, the total weight of items can be easily calculated. The extension activity involves the children beginning to appreciate that 500 g is half a kilogram and that 1000 g is one kilogram.

SUGGESTED QUESTIONS:

- How many grams is the same as a kilogram?
- How many grams is the same as half a kilogram?
- Which pictures show things that are heavier/lighter than half a kilogram?

## Capacity cards (page 45)

Begin by showing the children a variety of litre containers of different shapes, for example tall and thin, short and wide, to help them make judgements about these pictures. Young children often confuse height with how much something holds, for example thinking that a tall thin container has a larger capacity than a short wide container. Discuss their decisions in the plenary session.

SUGGESTED QUESTIONS:

- Which of these two containers do you think holds more? Does your partner agree?
- Which ones are you unsure about?

## Litre checker (page 46)

At the start of the lesson, give each group of children a litre container full of water and different containers to compare it with. They could test which of the containers holds more or less than one litre by pouring water into them. If your school has large plant pots and tubs, discuss with the children whether these would hold more than, less than or exactly one litre.

SOLUTIONS:

| | |
|---|---|
| More than one litre | Less than one litre |
| Less than one litre | Less than one litre |
| More than one litre | More than one litre |
| Less than one litre | More than one litre |

SUGGESTED QUESTION:

- Which object do you think holds the most/least?

## Read the numbered divisions on a scale, and interpret the divisions between them, for example on a scale from 0 to 25 with intervals of 1 shown but only the divisions 0, 5, 10, 15 and 20 numbered; use a ruler to draw and measure lines to the nearest centimetre

It is important that the children become familiar with different types of scale on a range of measuring instruments and begin to learn how to interpret the reading. Initially the

children should read from scales where all divisions are numbered and then should move on to those where the interval marks are shown but not numbered. This requires them to work out what each unnumbered mark represents. As they first encounter this work, the unnumbered marks represent one unit and numbered divisions may go up in 2s, 5s or even 10s. Another aspect of reading scales is realising that amounts can be slightly above or below a mark. Vocabulary such as 'about', 'almost', 'just under', 'just over' is also important for children of this age.

The children should now be becoming familiar with rulers and be learning to draw and measure different lengths of line (whole centimetres).

## Scale trail (page 47)

Ensure that children understand the rules for this activity. When the scale is read, the number of kilograms shown becomes the number of positions down the track that the counter is moved. The scale landed on is then read and the activity continues to the winning sections. Different starting points can be explored.

SOLUTIONS:

Starting point A: computer
Starting point B: scooter
Starting point C: bike

SUGGESTED QUESTIONS:

- What mass does this scale show?
- Which number comes between 2 and 4?

## Monster weights (page 48)

This activity contains scales with numbered divisions going up in 5s. The arrows could be masked and altered to provide more variety or the numbers could be changed as appropriate, for example going up in 10s.

Solutions:

| | | |
|---|---|---|
| 11 kg | 18 kg | 3 kg |
| 8 kg | 17 kg | 13 kg |

SUGGESTED QUESTIONS:

- Which monster is the heaviest/lightest?
- How much heavier is this monster than this one?

## Deep water (page 49)

This sheet explores some of the vocabulary related to non-exact readings on a simple scale.

SUGGESTED QUESTIONS:

- Does your picture show more or less than 3 litres? Is either correct?

## Dizzy the baker: 1 and 2 (pages 50–51)

Hold up a real kitchen timer and discuss what it is used for. These two activity sheets show scales with intervals of 1 but only the divisions 0, 5, 10, 15 and 20... numbered. The first sheet shows times up to 25 minutes and the second sheet shows times up to 1 hour (60 minutes).

**SUGGESTED QUESTIONS:**

- How many minutes does this timer show?
- Which cake matches which timer?

## Flea party (page 52)

For this activity, the children can draw lines between any pair of fleas and measure and record the length. Demonstrate how to use a ruler to measure the length of a line, positioning the ruler correctly at one end of the line. Encourage the children to compare answers with a partner and see if they have measured any of the same lines. Use a range of vocabulary when discussing the distances between fleas such as in the questions below.

**SUGGESTED QUESTIONS:**

- How far is flea A from flea D? Are the fleas close together or far apart?
- How many centimetres away from flea G is flea D?
- Is flea E more than 10 centimetres from flea B?
- How far would flea F need to walk in a straight line to reach flea C?

## Spaghetti spikes (page 53)

Provide small pieces of string for the extension activity and demonstrate how string and a ruler can be used to find the length of non-straight lengths.

**SOLUTIONS:**

10 cm
12 cm       15 cm
9 cm        5 cm

**NOW TRY THIS!**

14 cm
13 cm       24 cm

**SUGGESTED QUESTIONS:**

- Where do you place your ruler when you measure a line?
- Is your little finger longer or shorter than the shortest line on the page?

## Frog tongues! (page 54)

Provide small pieces of string for the extension activity and demonstrate how string and a ruler can be used to find the length of non-straight lengths. Children could check each other's work by measuring the lengths of all the frog tongues on a partner's sheet.

**SUGGESTED QUESTIONS:**

- How much longer does this line have to be to reach the fly?
- What is the longest tongue that your ruler could measure?

## Ant trail (page 55)

As children become more confident in measuring the lengths of straight lines they can begin to explore early ideas of perimeter, found by measuring each side and then finding the total of all the lengths.

**SOLUTIONS:**

22 cm       24 cm
            24 cm
26 cm       26 cm

**SUGGESTED QUESTIONS:**

- How far around the whole shape will the ant travel?
- What is the length/width of this rectangle?
- What do you notice about how long these two opposite sides are? Is this always true?

## Use units of time (seconds, minutes, hours, days) and know the relationships between them; read the time to the quarter hour; identify time intervals, including those that cross the hour

Words that children should begin to develop an understanding of, and begin to use themselves in everyday language, include:

*time, days of the week: Monday, Tuesday etc.*
*months of the year: January, February, March etc.*
*day, week, birthday, holiday, morning, afternoon,*
*evening, night, bedtime, dinnertime, playtime,*
*today, yesterday, tomorrow, before, after,*
*next, last, now, soon, early, late, earlier, later,*
*quick, quicker, quickest, quickly, first,*
*slow, slower, slowest, slowly,*
*old, older, oldest, new, newer, newest,*
*takes longer, takes less time, hour, o'clock,*
*clock, watch, hands, half past, quarter past, 15 minutes past,*
*thirty minutes past, quarter to, forty-five, 15 minutes to...*

As the children begin to learn to tell the time to the quarter of an hour on analogue clocks (those with faces) they can begin to be shown how these times are represented by :00, :15, :30 and :45 on digital clocks with the hour past preceding the colon.

Children should also begin to appreciate time intervals, such as saying what time it will be in half an hour, or saying the length of time between two given times.

## Fun time (page 56)

Provide some similar oral activities before the children begin this sheet. Discuss classroom activities and say whether they take seconds, minutes or hours. Ask them to make an estimate as to exactly how long each activity takes, for example: taking the register – 4 minutes.

**SOLUTIONS:**

hour
minutes
minutes
seconds
minutes
minutes
minutes
hours

**SUGGESTED QUESTION:**

• Do you think it will take 5 seconds, 5 minutes or 5 hours?

## Charlie and Chester (page 57)

This activity involves appreciating the relationship between seconds, minutes and hours. Following a class discussion, write a list of the relationships on the board for children to refer to, for example:

1 minute = 60 seconds
1 hour = 60 minutes
1 day = 24 hours

**SOLUTIONS:**

Chester
Charlie
Chester
Chester
Charlie
Charlie
Chester

**NOW TRY THIS!**

Charlie

**SUGGESTED QUESTIONS:**

• How can you work out whether 1 hour or 65 minutes is longer?
• How many seconds are there in 2 minutes?

## Wally's wonder watch: 1 and 2 (pages 58–59)

These two sheets involve analogue clocks (clock-faces). The first involves reading the time in words and drawing it on the clock-face. The second involves reading the time on the clock-face and writing the time shown in words. Discuss with the children that the time in words can be written in different ways and that these are all correct, for example three-fifteen or quarter past three or 15 minutes past three.

**SUGGESTED QUESTIONS:**

• What time does this clock show?
• Which number is the short hand, the hour hand, pointing to?
• How could you show 5 o'clock?
• Which number would the short hand be pointing to?

## Carol's classy clock: 1 and 2 (pages 60–61)

These two sheets explore digital clocks and time.

The first involves reading the time in words and writing it on the digital clock. The second involves reading the time on the digital clock and writing the time shown in words. Encourage the children to use the words 'quarter to/past', 'o'clock' and 'half past' for the latter activity. At the start of the activities show how 'o'clock' times are represented by :00 on digital clocks and that :30 represents half past, or 30 minutes past; :15 quarter past and :45 quarter to, and so on. Explain also that the hour always comes first in digital clock times, for example 6:30 means half past 6. It is common for children to reverse these times, showing it as 30:6 as this more closely matches the way 30 minutes past 6 or half past 6 is written and spoken.

**SUGGESTED QUESTIONS:**

• What time does this clock show?
• Which number tells you the hour?
• What does :45 mean?
• How could you show 5 o'clock? Half past 4?

## TV times: 1 and 2 (pages 62–63)

Provide the children with clocks with moveable hands to help them with the following activities. They should move the hands from one time to the other and work out how long has passed.

**SUGGESTED QUESTIONS:**

• How long do you have to wait until the cartoons begin? How could you say that in a different way?
• How many minutes are between 2 o'clock and quarter past 2?

## Time quiz (page 64)

The times on this sheet could be altered before copying to provide further practice. If the children are experiencing difficulty with this sheet showing digital times, give small analogue clocks to the children and ask them to make the correct time and then turn the hand backwards or forwards to answer the question. Note that it is preferable to have clocks where the hour hand correctly moves as the minute hand is turned.

**SOLUTIONS:**

| | |
|---|---|
| **c** 8:30 | **d** 5:00 |
| **c** 3:15 | **c** 12:30 |
| **c** 9:30 | **d** 6:30 |
| **c** 5:30 | **b** 7:45 |

**SUGGESTED QUESTIONS:**

• What time does this clock show?
• Can you show me this time on the clock-face?

# Using the CD-ROM

The PC CD-ROM included with this book contains an easy-to-use software program that allows you to print out pages from the book, to view them (e.g. on an interactive whiteboard) or to customise the activities to suit the needs of your pupils.

## Getting started

It's easy to run the software. Simply insert the CD-ROM into your CD drive and the disk should autorun and launch the interface in your web browser.

If the disk does not autorun, open 'My Computer' and select the CD drive, then open the file 'start.html'.

Please note: this CD-ROM is designed for use on a PC. It will also run on most Apple Macintosh computers in Safari however, due to the differences between Mac and PC fonts, you may experience some unavoidable variations in the typography and page layouts of the activity sheets.

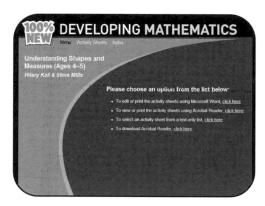

## The Menu screen

Four options are available to you from the main menu screen.

The first option takes you to the Activity Sheets screen, where you can choose an activity sheet to edit or print out using Microsoft Word.

(If you do not have the Microsoft Office suite, you might like to consider using OpenOffice instead. This is a multi-platform and multi-lingual office suite, and an 'open-source' project. It is compatible with all other major office suites, and the product is free to download, use and distribute. The homepage for OpenOffice on the Internet is: www.openoffice.org.)

The second option on the main menu screen opens a PDF file of the entire book using Adobe Reader (see below). This format is ideal for printing out copies of the activity sheets or for displaying them, for example on an interactive whiteboard.

The third option allows you to choose a page to edit from a text-only list of the activity sheets, as an alternative to the graphical interface on the Activity Sheets screen.

Adobe Reader is free to download and to use. If it is not already installed on your computer, the fourth link takes you to the download page on the Adobe website.

You can also navigate directly to any of the three screens at any time by using the tabs at the top.

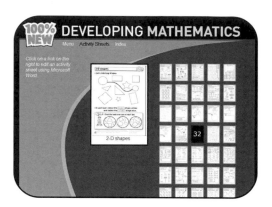

## The Activity Sheets screen

This screen shows thumbnails of all the activity sheets in the book. Rolling the mouse over a thumbnail highlights the page number and also brings up a preview image of the page.

Click on the thumbnail to open a version of the page in Microsoft Word (or an equivalent software program, see above.) The full range of editing tools are available to you here to customise the page to suit the needs of your particular pupils. You can print out copies of the page or save a copy of your edited version onto your computer.

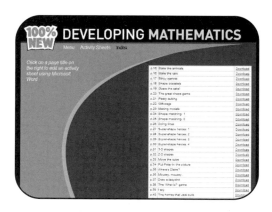

## The Index screen

This is a text-only version of the Activity Sheets screen described above. Choose an activity sheet and click on the 'download' link to open a version of the page in Microsoft Word to edit or print out.

## Technical support

If you have any questions regarding the *100% New Developing Literacy* or *Developing Mathematics* software, please email us at the address below. We will get back to you as quickly as possible.

educationalsales@acblack.com

# Spot the shapes

• Colour the 3 shapes that have been used to make each design.

Teachers' note This activity helps the children to become more visually perceptive and to identify several shapes overlapping. This is an important skill that some children find difficult. Once they have identified the shapes in the designs, discuss their properties, making reference to numbers of sides, whether they are straight or curved, number of right angles and so on.

100% New Developing Mathematics
Understanding Shapes and
Measures: Ages 6–7
© A & C BLACK

# Sticky labels

- **Use the price list to find the cost of each pack of sticky labels.**
- **You may use a price more than once.**

£4.50

| Price list | |
|---|---|
| Circle | £4.80 |
| Rectangle | £3.00 |
| Pentagon | £3.90 |
| Triangle | £4.50 |
| Hexagon | £5.20 |
| Square | £3.80 |
| Octagon | £4.30 |

**NOW TRY THIS!**

- **Ring any right angles that you can see on the stickers above.**

**Teachers' note** Discuss the names and properties of the 2-D shapes before beginning this activity. Encourage the children to count the number of straight sides making up the shapes and to find the name of the shape in the list that has that number of sides.

**100% New Developing Mathematics
Understanding Shapes and
Measures: Ages 6–7
© A & C BLACK**

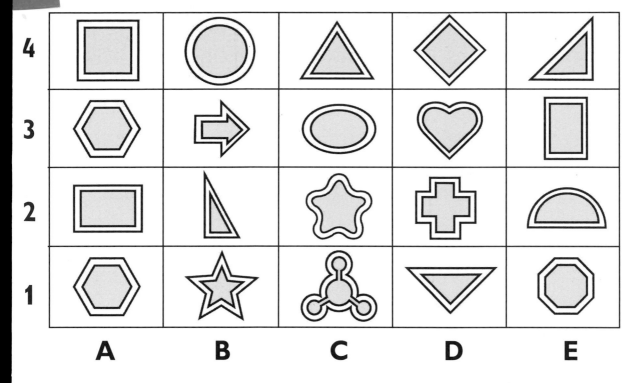

|  | A | B | C | D | E |

**A**    **B**    **C**    **D**    **E**

• Tick ⬚ true or ⬚ false for each statement.

**D4** contains a square.
[✔] true   [ ] false

**Row 3** contains a triangle.
[ ] true   [ ] false

**Column A** contains two hexagons.
[ ] true   [ ] false

**B2** contains a triangle.
[ ] true   [ ] false

**A2** and **E3** are the same shape.
[ ] true   [ ] false

**E1** contains a pentagon.
[ ] true   [ ] false

**B4** contains a shape with 1 side.
[ ] true   [ ] false

**B3** contains a hexagon.
[ ] true   [ ] false

**NOW TRY THIS!**

• Write 4 true statements of your own.

Teachers' note This activity provides revision of shape names and properties and also explores using letters and numbers to represent positions of items in a grid formation.

100% New Developing Mathematics Understanding Shapes and Measures: Ages 6–7 © A & C BLACK

# Open up: 1

These shapes have been folded in half along the dotted line.

- **Write how many sides you think each shape will have when opened out.**

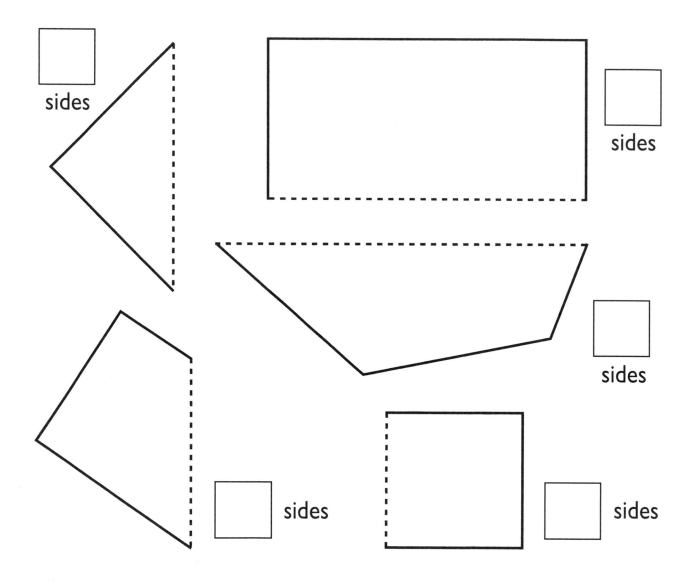

sides

sides

sides

sides

sides

**NOW TRY THIS!**

- **Fold a piece of paper and cut out your own shape.**
- **Ask a partner to guess how many sides the shape has when opened out.**

**Teachers' note** This sheet should be used in conjunction with the following sheet. First give out this sheet and ask children to predict the number of sides of the shapes when opened out. Then provide the solutions on the following page and ask children to cut out the shapes and to fold and open them to check their own answers.

**100% New Developing Mathematic
Understanding Shapes and
Measures: Ages 6–7
© A & C BLACK**

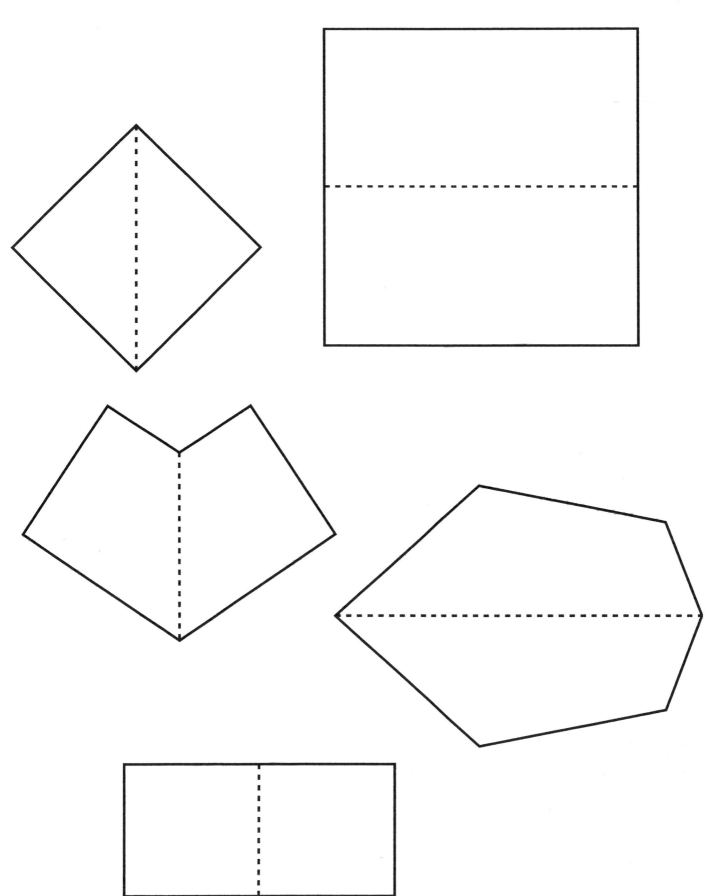

**Teachers' note** This sheet should be used in conjunction with the previous sheet. First give out that sheet and ask children to predict the number of sides of the shapes when opened up. Then provide the solutions on this page and ask children to cut out the shapes and to fold and open them to check their own answers.

**100% New Developing Mathematics
Understanding Shapes and
Measures: Ages 6–7**
© A & C BLACK

# shape speedway!

- Play this game with a partner. You need a dice, a counter and a small mirror each.

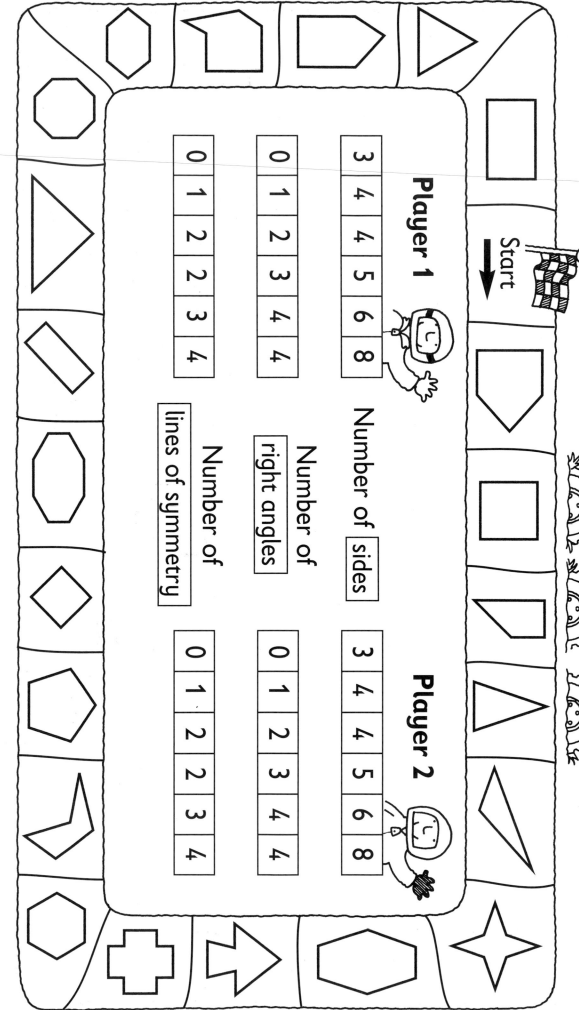

Start ↓

## Player 1

**Number of sides**

| 3 | 4 | 4 | 5 | 6 | 8 |
|---|---|---|---|---|---|

**Number of right angles**

| 0 | 1 | 2 | 3 | 4 | 4 |
|---|---|---|---|---|---|

**Number of lines of symmetry**

| 0 | 1 | 2 | 2 | 3 | 4 |
|---|---|---|---|---|---|

## Player 2

**Number of sides**

| 3 | 4 | 4 | 5 | 6 | 8 |
|---|---|---|---|---|---|

**Number of right angles**

| 0 | 1 | 2 | 3 | 4 | 4 |
|---|---|---|---|---|---|

**Number of lines of symmetry**

| 0 | 1 | 2 | 2 | 3 | 4 |
|---|---|---|---|---|---|

**Teachers' note** The children take turns to roll the dice and move their counter. The shape landed on should be examined for numbers of sides, right angles and lines of symmetry. The children should colour any numbers that they can in the centre. The game ends after a given number of laps. The winner is the player with the most coloured at the end of the game.

100% New Developing Mathematics
Understanding Shapes and
Measures: Ages 6–7
© A & C BLACK

# Crazy colours

## You need coloured pencils for this activity.

Tick red: any cubes

Tick blue: any shape with a circular face

Tick green: shapes that have triangular faces

Tick yellow: shapes that have no flat faces

Tick pink: any shapes with only rectangular faces

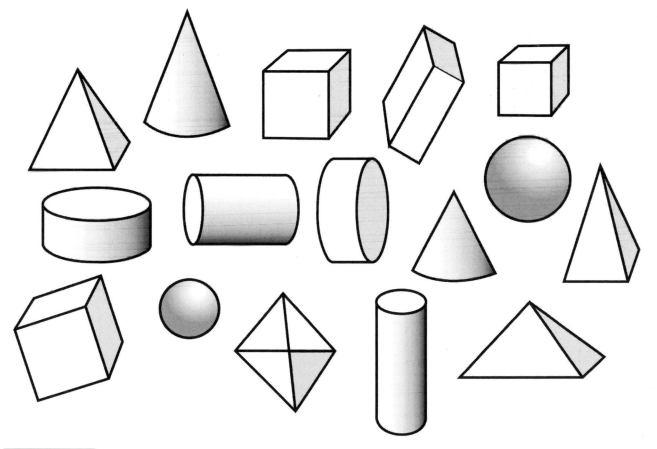

**NOW TRY THIS!**

• **Draw a ring around any shapes above that have 8 corners.**

**Teachers' note** Ensure that the children have coloured pencils to match the colours shown. (These can be altered before copying.) Provide the children with matching solid shapes to enable them to count and examine the properties.

**100% New Developing Mathematics Understanding Shapes and Measures: Ages 6–7**
© A & C BLACK

# Solids speedway!

100% New Developing Mathematic
Understanding Shapes and
Measures: Ages 6–7
© A & C BLACK

- Play this game with a partner. You need a dice and a counter each.

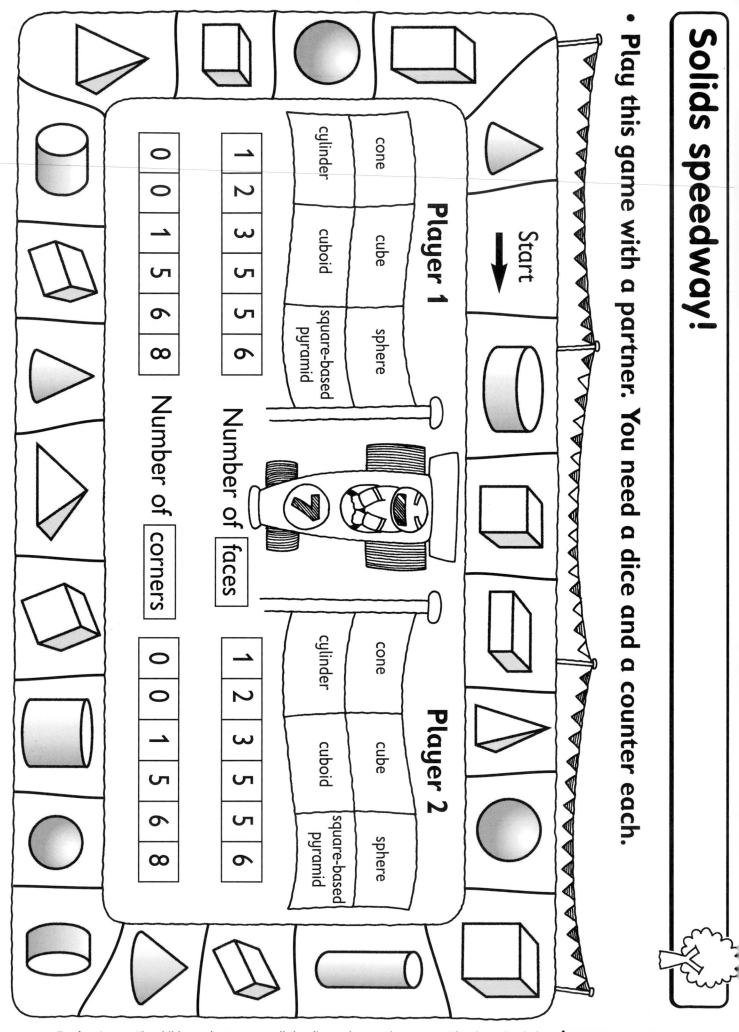

Start ↓

## Player 1

| cone | cube | sphere |
|---|---|---|
| cylinder | cuboid | square-based pyramid |

Number of faces

| 1 | 2 | 3 | 5 | 5 | 6 |
|---|---|---|---|---|---|
| 0 | 0 | 1 | 5 | 6 | 8 |

Number of corners

## Player 2

| cone | cube | sphere |
|---|---|---|
| cylinder | cuboid | square-based pyramid |

Number of faces

| 1 | 2 | 3 | 5 | 5 | 6 |
|---|---|---|---|---|---|
| 0 | 0 | 1 | 5 | 6 | 8 |

Number of corners

**Teachers' note** The children take turns to roll the dice and move the counter. The shape landed on should be named and examined for number of faces and vertices (corners). The children should colour any names and numbers that they can in the centre. The game ends after a given number of laps. The winner is the player with the most coloured at the end of the game.

# Guess the shape

- **Cut out the cards.**
- **Use the clues to help you guess each 3-D shape.**
- **Draw a picture of the shape on the back of the card.**

It has 8 corners.

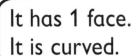

It has 1 face.
It is curved.

It has 12 edges all the same length.
Its faces are square.

All of its faces are triangles.

One of its faces is square. The rest are triangles.

It has 1 corner and 1 edge.

It has 2 curved edges.

All of its faces are rectangles.

**NOW TRY THIS!**

- **Make up new clues for these shapes.**

  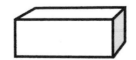 

**Teachers' note** Provide the children with a set of 3-D shapes, including sphere, cone, cylinder, cube, cuboid, square-based pyramid and tetrahedron (triangular-based pyramid).

*100% New Developing Mathematics Understanding Shapes and Measures: Ages 6–7 © A & C BLACK*

# Exercise pairs

**Teachers' note** Explain to the children that these acrobats are working in pairs. One person in each pair is using their body to show a reflection of their partner's body. Ask the children to cut out the cards and match them. As an extension activity the children could draw their own pairs of exercise cards, showing bodies and their reflections.

**100% New Developing Mathematics
Understanding Shapes and
Measures: Ages 6–7
© A & C BLACK**

# Mirror mania

Ella holds some cards next to a mirror.

- **Colour the cards using at least 3 different colours so that the mirror shows the reflection each time.**

**NOW TRY THIS!**

- **Draw the reflection of the shape of this card and colour it.**

**Teachers' note** Provide the children with mirrors of their own to test and check their reflections. Demonstrate how to hold the mirror next to the shape and then how to lift it to check whether their answer underneath is correct.

**100% New Developing Mathematics Understanding Shapes and Measures: Ages 6–7 © A & C BLACK**

# Snip, snip

**Josh has made these** ⟨symmetrical⟩ **shapes by folding and cutting paper.**

• **Draw a line on each shape to show where he folded them.**

 **NOW TRY THIS!**

• **Make 4 shapes of your own by folding and cutting paper.**

**Teachers' note** Demonstrate how to fold a piece of paper in half and then how to cut and open it out to make a complete shape. Explain that the fold line is known as the 'mirror line' or the 'line of symmetry'.

100% New Developing Mathematics
Understanding Shapes and
Measures: Ages 6–7
© A & C BLACK

# Paper shapes

Some children are making paper shapes.
Each child folds their piece of paper in half.

- Colour the shapes that could be made by
  each piece of paper if it is folded in half.
  There can be more than one answer.

## NOW TRY THIS!

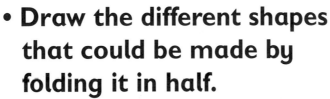

- Cut out this shape.
- Draw the different shapes
  that could be made by
  folding it in half.

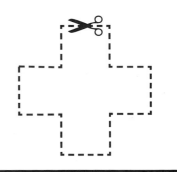

**Teachers' note** If some children are finding this activity difficult, it might be useful to enlarge the sheet to A3 so that those children can cut out each shape and fold it in half to see which of the shapes can be made.

100% New Developing Mathematics
Understanding Shapes and
Measures: Ages 6–7
© A & C BLACK

• **Cut out the pictures at the bottom of the sheet.**

• **Arrange the pictures onto the grid so that all these statements are true.**

The chest is to the left of the volcano.

The bridge is to the right of the volcano.

The flag is above the chest.

The cave is above the volcano.

The cannon is between the cave and the ship.

The skull is below the ship.

The tree is above the ship.

The parrot is next to the tree.

The hut is between the anchor and the parrot.

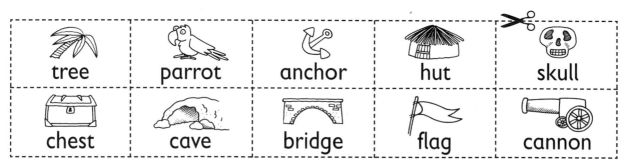

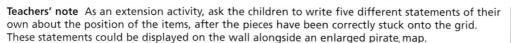

Teachers' note As an extension activity, ask the children to write five different statements of their own about the position of the items, after the pieces have been correctly stuck onto the grid. These statements could be displayed on the wall alongside an enlarged pirate map.

100% New Developing Mathematics
Understanding Shapes and
Measures: Ages 6–7
© A & C BLACK

- **Follow the instructions. Start at the arrow each time.**
- **Colour to show who sits where.**

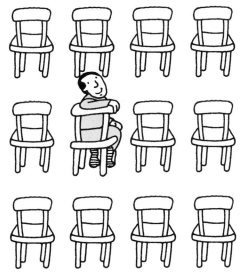

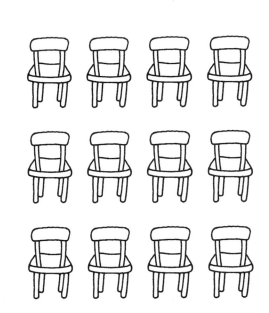

Enter the hall.

**Mr Green**  Go straight until you reach the **third row** of chairs.
Turn ⌈left⌉ and sit in the **second** chair.

**Mrs Black**  Go straight until you reach the **second row** of chairs.
Turn ⌈right⌉ and sit in the **fourth** chair.

**Ms Yellow**  Turn ⌈left⌉ when you reach the **first row** of chairs.
Sit in the **third** chair.

**Mr Blue**  Go straight until you reach the **third row** of chairs.
Turn ⌈right⌉ and sit in the **first** chair.

**Mrs Red**  Go straight until you reach the **second row** of chairs.
Turn ⌈left⌉ and sit in the **fourth** chair.

**NOW TRY THIS!**

## Mr Grey is already seated.
- **Write directions for how he reached his seat.**

**Teachers' note** This activity encourages the children to follow directions and begin to use the words 'left' and 'right' correctly. If necessary the words 'left' and 'right' can be written on the sheet with arrows for those children who are finding it difficult.

**100% New Developing Mathematics
Understanding Shapes and
Measures: Ages 6–7
© A & C BLACK**

29

# In the kitchen

- **Look at the items on these shelves.**
- **Complete the sentences using any word or phrase from the word-bank.**

## Word-bank

| to the left of | next to | between |
| lower than | opposite | underneath |
| to the right of | above | beside |
| higher than | far from | below |

1. The shampoo is _____ the beans.

2. The milk is _____ the coffee.

3. The cereal is _____ the tissues.

4. The beans are _____ the tissues.

5. The tissues are _____ the milk.

6. The milk is _____ the coffee and the beans.

7. The cereal is _____ the coffee.

8. The shampoo is _____ the tissues.

**NOW TRY THIS!**

- **Write 4 more sentences of your own using any words or phrases you haven't used.**

**Teachers' note** Children can be asked further questions about the positions of the items. Encourage them to see opposites, for example that if the milk is to the right of the beans, then the beans are to the left of the milk. The children can collect a list of position words for display.

100% New Developing Mathematics
Understanding Shapes and
Measures: Ages 6–7
© A & C BLACK

# Avoid the zombies

- ## Work with a partner.

☆ Take it in turns to place a counter at the start.

☆ Move to the finish avoiding all the zombies.

☆ Describe the route to your partner.

Use these words.

**Word-bank**

left ⬅

right ➡

up ⬆

down ⬇

- ## With your partner, write a list of instructions to show 3 different routes.

'Right 1' means 'move right 1 square'.

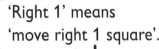

| Route 1 | Route 2 | Route 3 |
|---------|---------|---------|
| right 1 | | |
| up 3 | | |
| | | |
| | | |
| | | |

**NOW TRY THIS!**

- **Draw Route 3 on the grid.**
- **Write the instructions going back from the** finish **to the** start .

**Teachers' note** An additional activity can be played with this maze. Give each pair a set of cards marked Left, Right, Up and Down and a counter each. The children should take it in turns to pick a card and, where possible, move in that direction until a zombie is reached. A target square can be agreed in advance and the winner is the first to reach it.

**100% New Developing Mathematics
Understanding Shapes and
Measures: Ages 6–7**
© A & C BLACK

# The hamster run

- **Work with a partner.**
- **Tell the story of where the hamster went.**
- **Use these words in your story.**

## Word-bank

left    right    under    over    between    up    down
round    through    along    beside    turn    straight

**Teachers' note** Before the children begin the activity, discuss what is happening in the illustration. The children can describe the journey to a partner or could record it on paper. Ensure the children understand that they can use more words than just those given in the word-bank.

100% New Developing Mathematics
Understanding Shapes and
Measures: Ages 6–7
© A & C BLACK

# Rotating pictures

**This picture has been turned** clockwise **through** a quarter turn **4 times.**

- **Draw what these pictures will look like if you do the same.**

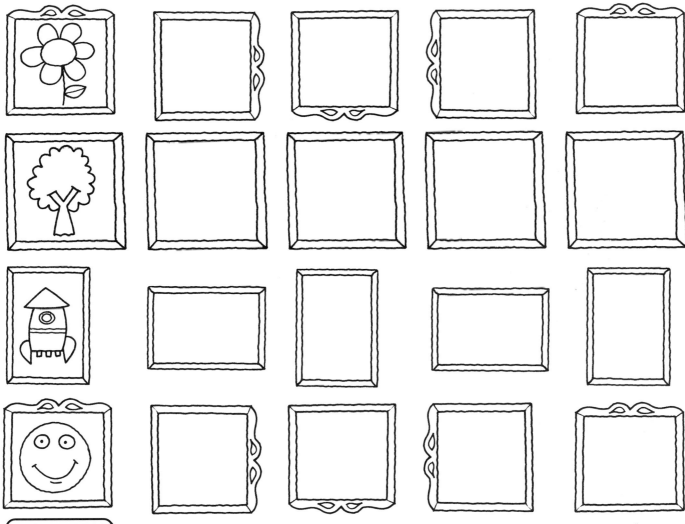

**NOW TRY THIS!**

- **On the back of the sheet draw a picture of your own and show** anticlockwise **quarter turns.**

**Teachers' note** Tracing paper could be used for this activity or the children could cut out the original picture and rotate it. Encourage them to appreciate that four quarter turns return the picture back to its original position. Children can be shown this function on a computer, for example using drawing tools in word-processing software.

*100% New Developing Mathematics*
**Understanding Shapes and**
**Measures: Ages 6–7**
© A & C BLACK

**33**

# In a spin

Beth is playing a turning game.
She makes turns to face different letters.

• **Write the words that she spells out.**

Face **m**

Make a half turn clockwise.

Make a quarter turn clockwise.

Make a half turn anticlockwise.

| m |
|---|
|   |
|   |
|   |

Beth spells

_____

---

Face **n**

Make a half turn clockwise.

Make a quarter turn clockwise.

Make a half turn anticlockwise.

|   |
|---|
|   |
|   |
|   |

Beth spells

_____

---

Face **m**

Make a quarter turn anticlockwise.

Make a half turn clockwise.

Make a quarter turn clockwise.

|   |
|---|
|   |
|   |
|   |

Beth spells

_____

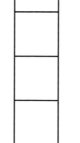

 **NOW TRY THIS!**

• **Write instructions for how to spell:**

man, men.

**Teachers' note** Draw attention to the fact that turning clockwise or anticlockwise through half a turn produces the same result.

**100% New Developing Mathematic Understanding Shapes and Measures: Ages 6–7**
© A & C BLACK

# Feeding time

- **Play this game with a partner.**

☆ Cut out the cards and place them face down.

☆ Take turns to pick a card and say what the angle is.

☆ If your partner agrees, score the points shown on the scoreboard above.

**Score**

| | |
|---|---|
| right angle | 5 points |
| **smaller** than a right angle | 1 point |
| **larger** than a right angle | 3 points |

Teachers' note See page 9 for an introductory activity to help the children to recognise right angles.

100% New Developing Mathematics
Understanding Shapes and
Measures: Ages 6–7
© A & C BLACK

# Hexagon handiwork

A hexagon has been drawn on the first grid.

• Draw a different hexagon on each grid.

NOW TRY THIS!

• Write how many right angles each hexagon has.

Teachers' note Remind the children that a closed shape with six sides is called a hexagon, so the shape on the sheet is a hexagon. For the extension activity ensure that children recognise right angles in different orientations, for example noticing that the first hexagon has two right angles.

100% New Developing Mathematic
Understanding Shapes and
Measures: Ages 6–7
© A & C BLACK

# Power-robots!

Here are drawings of 2 power-robots.

- Carefully cut out the right-angle gobbler from the bottom of the page.
- Use it to find which power-robot has more right angles.
- Mark each right angle like this.

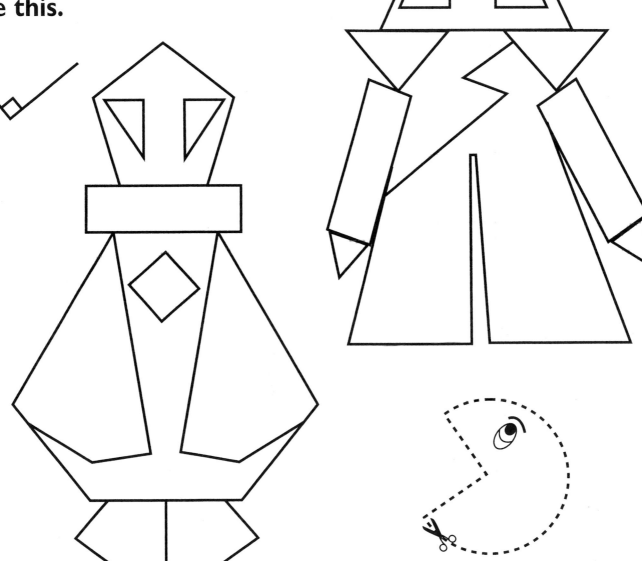

**NOW TRY THIS!**

- Write how many right angles each hexagon has.

**Teachers' note** At the start of the lesson, demonstrate how to use the right-angle gobbler to test angles. Ensure the children realise that they need to line up one edge of its 'mouth' with a line or edge and make sure that where the two lines or edges join is at the corner of its 'mouth'.

*100% New Developing Mathematics*
**Understanding Shapes and Measures: Ages 6–7**
© A & C BLACK

**37**

# The metre beater game

- **Play this game with a partner.**

> You need some counters.

☆ Cut out the cards and place them face down on the table.

☆ Each player picks a card. If the length on the card is longer than a metre the player collects a counter.

☆ Also, the player that has the longer length of the two collects a counter.

☆ Put the cards to one side and pick 2 new cards.

☆ Continue playing until all the cards have been used.

| | | |
|---|---|---|
| 1 metre | 20 centimetres | 150 centimetres |
| 1 metre and 10 centimetres | 80 centimetres | 99 centimetres |
| 1 metre and 5 centimetres | 60 centimetres | 110 centimetres |
| 1 metre and 30 centimetres | 40 centimetres | 120 centimetres |
| 2 metres | 6 centimetres | 300 centimetres |
| 1 metre and 99 centimetres | 9 centimetres | 87 centimetres |
| 4 metres | 50 centimetres | 199 centimetres |
| 2 metres and 50 centimetres | 66 centimetres | 180 centimetres |

**Teachers' note** These cards can be used for a range of comparing activities, such as the following: individual children can pick two cards, say which is longer and record them using the < or > signs; pairs of children can pick a card and then use rulers and a metre stick to draw that length along the playground in chalk. Further ideas can be found on page 9.

100% New Developing Mathematic
Understanding Shapes and
Measures: Ages 6–7
© A & C BLACK

# Going to great lengths

- **You can use** ⌗centimetres⌗ **or** ⌗metres⌗ **to measure these things. Write which is best.**

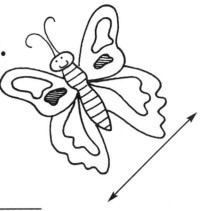

**1.** length of
a lorry

metres
_____

**2.** width of
a butterfly

_____

**3.** length of
a rabbit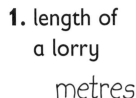

_____

**4.** height of
a house

_____

**5.** width of
a laptop

_____

**6.** depth of
a bucket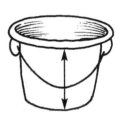

_____

**7.** length of
the school hall

_____

**8.** height of
a lamp post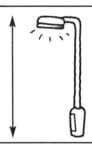

_____

**9.** thickness of
a book

_____

**10.** distance from
our playground
to the school hall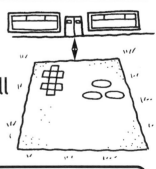

_____

**NOW TRY THIS!**

- **Draw 4 other things you would measure in metres or centimetres.**

**Teachers' note** Encourage the children to realise that the words 'length', 'width', 'height', 'depth', 'thickness' and 'distance' all refer to types of length that can be measured in centimetres or metres.

**100% New Developing Mathematics
Understanding Shapes and
Measures: Ages 6–7
© A & C BLACK**

# Snail race

Each of these tables is ⌈ 1 metre ⌉ in length.
The snails race from one side of the table to the other.

- Estimate how many centimetres each snail has travelled across its table in 20 minutes.

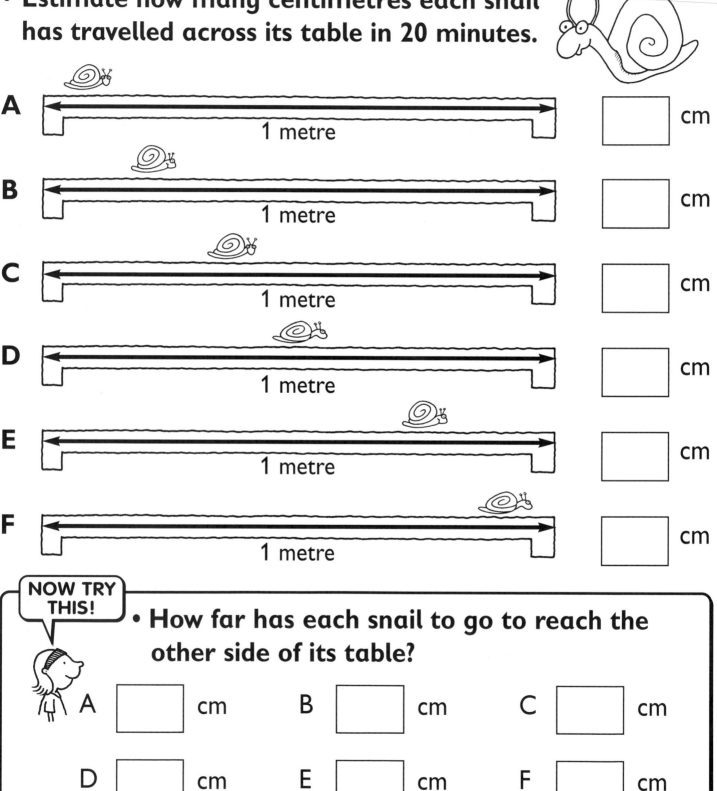

A ← 1 metre → ☐ cm

B ← 1 metre → ☐ cm

C ← 1 metre → ☐ cm

D ← 1 metre → ☐ cm

E ← 1 metre → ☐ cm

F ← 1 metre → ☐ cm

**NOW TRY THIS!**

- How far has each snail to go to reach the other side of its table?

A ☐ cm   B ☐ cm   C ☐ cm

D ☐ cm   E ☐ cm   F ☐ cm

**Teachers' note** Ensure the children realise that they should look at what proportion of the 1-metre length each snail has travelled and then estimate about how many centimetres this would be. Provide metre sticks so that the children do not confuse the length of the drawing itself with the 1-metre length in real life.

**100% New Developing Mathematics**
Understanding Shapes and
Measures: Ages 6–7
© A & C BLACK

# Crunchy carrots

- ## Play this game with a partner.

☆ Take turns to choose a carrot.

☆ Estimate its length in centimetres. Your partner checks your estimate by measuring the carrot with a ruler.

☆ Score 2 points if you are exactly right and 1 point if your estimate was only 1 centimetre away.

☆ The winner is the player with the highest score at the end.

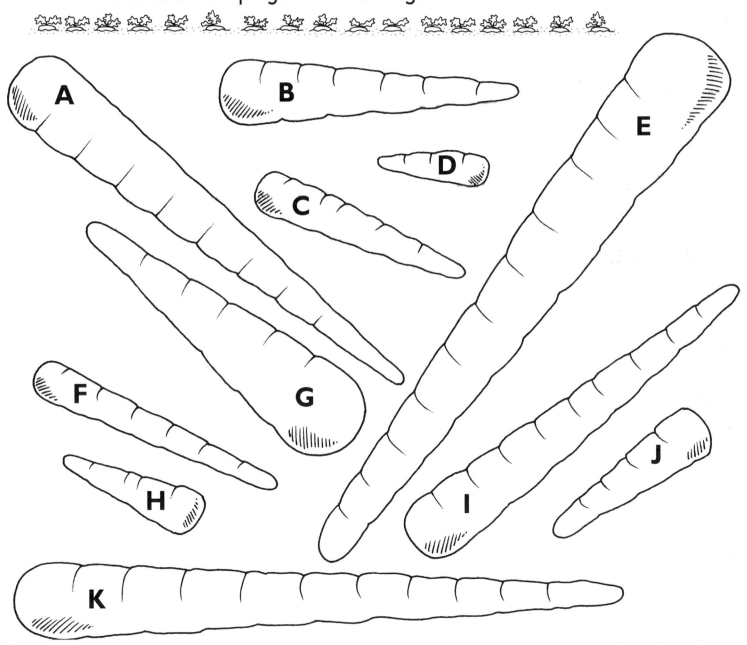

**Teachers' note** Ask the children to record the letter of the carrot, the estimate and the actual length. This could be drawn as a table on the board at the start of the lesson for them to copy and complete. As an extension activity, the children could be asked to list the carrots in order of size, starting with the smallest.

100% New Developing Mathematics
Understanding Shapes and
Measures: Ages 6–7
© A & C BLACK

# Doggy differences

- ## Cut out these cards and work with a partner.

| Jack Russell | Chihuahua | Yorkshire Terrier | Corgi |
|---|---|---|---|
| 5 kg | 2 kg | 3 kg | 11 kg |
| St Bernard | Dachshund | Border Collie | Great Dane |
| 80 kg | 9 kg | 18 kg | 52 kg |
| Labrador Retriever | Boxer | German Shepherd | Cocker Spaniel |
| 30 kg | 32 kg | 38 kg | 12 kg |
| Scottish Terrier | Miniature Poodle | Irish Wolfhound | Pug |
| 8 kg | 7 kg | 50 kg | 6 kg |

**Teachers' note** Children can play a simple game in pairs, where they place the cards face down and pick one each. The difference between the two weights can be found and the player with the larger weight wins the cards. Alternatively, the cards can be used in conjunction with the following sheet and some kilogram weights.

**100% New Developing Mathematics Understanding Shapes and Measures: Ages 6–7** © A & C BLACK

# Doggy dilemmas

- **You need the cards from the 'Doggy differences' sheet. This is a kilogram weight.** [ ]
- **Use the cards to help you work out which scales will balance. Tick or cross to show whether they balance.**

**NOW TRY THIS!**

- **Use the cards to find more sets that balance.**
- **Draw two of them on the back of this sheet.**

**Teachers' note** Encourage the children to use the cards to find the weights and to work out which balance. Provide kilogram weights so that the children can feel how heavy some of the smaller dogs are and find items in the classroom that are about the same weight as some of the dogs.

**100% New Developing Mathematics Understanding Shapes and Measures: Ages 6–7**
**© A & C BLACK**

# Marble mania

- **A small marble weighs 5 g**

- **A large marble weighs 50 g**

- **A glass jar weighs 500 g**

- **Write the total weight of the items on each card.**

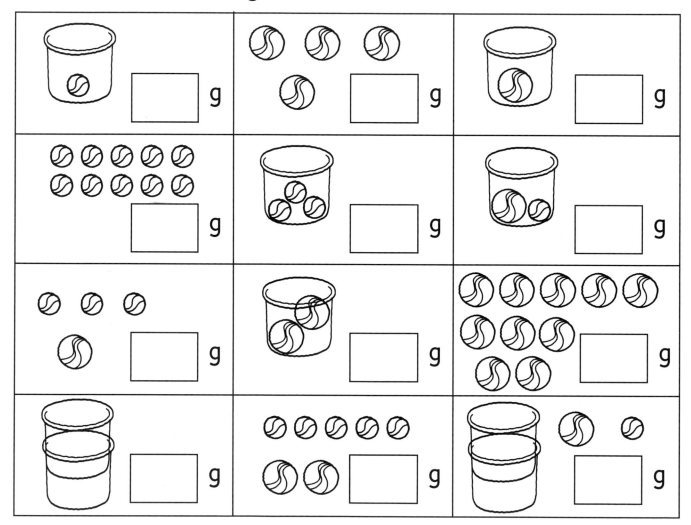

**NOW TRY THIS!**

- **Cut out the cards and put them in order of weight, starting with the lightest.**
- **Which are lighter than half a kilogram?**
- **Which are heavier than half a kilogram?**

**Teachers' note** Invite the children to say which picture shows a weight greater than one kilogram and ask them to write the amount in different ways, such as in kilograms and grams or just in grams. Encourage the children to weigh objects such as marbles practically to reinforce this activity.

**100% New Developing Mathematics**
Understanding Shapes and
Measures: Ages 6–7
© A & C BLACK

# Capacity cards

- ## Work with a partner and cut out the cards.

☆ Pick 2 cards and say which container you think holds more.

☆ If you are not sure, swap one of the cards.

☆ Stick them onto paper like this. holds more than

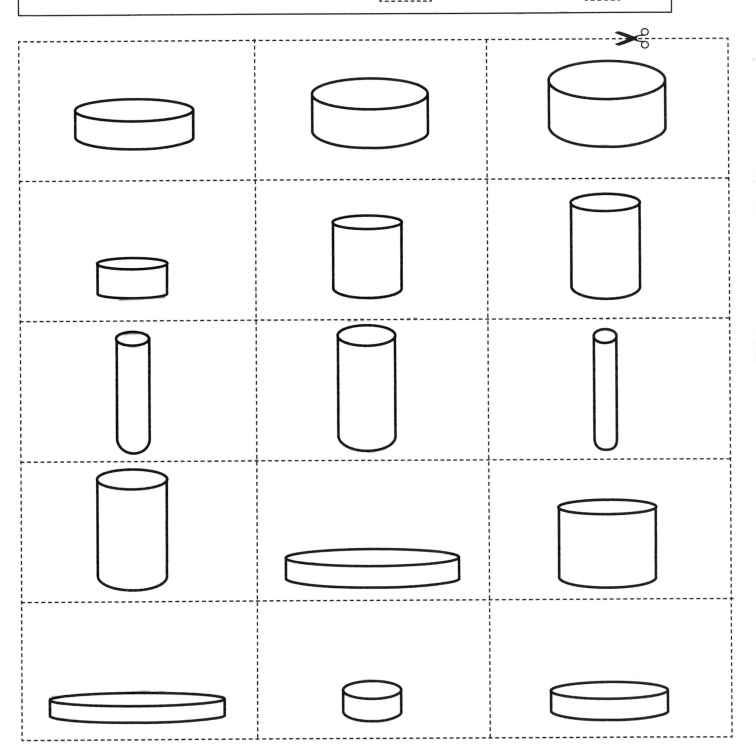

**Teachers' note** Encourage the children to appreciate that capacity does not directly correspond to height, for example a tall thin container can have a smaller capacity than a shorter, wider one. Provide practical equipment for the children to experiment with to support this work.

**100% New Developing Mathematics
Understanding Shapes and
Measures: Ages 6–7**
© A & C BLACK

45

# Litre checker

• **Tick whether each container in real life holds**
  more **or** less **than 1 litre.**

☑ more than 1 litre

☐ less than 1 litre

☐ more than 1 litre

☐ less than 1 litre

☐ more than 1 litre

☐ less than 1 litre

☐ more than 1 litre

☐ less than 1 litre

☐ more than 1 litre

☐ less than 1 litre

☐ more than 1 litre

☐ less than 1 litre

☐ more than 1 litre

☐ less than 1 litre

☐ more than 1 litre

☐ less than 1 litre

**NOW TRY THIS!**

• **Draw pictures of other items that,
  in real life, hold:** more than 1 kilogram

  less than 1 kilogram

---

**Teachers' note** Ensure that children are introduced to 1-litre containers and that they begin to appreciate their size. Support this activity with practical measuring using sand or water containers.

**100% New Developing Mathematics
Understanding Shapes and
Measures: Ages 6–7**
© A & C BLACK

# Scale trail

• **You need a counter for this activity.**

☆ Place your counter on the trail under A, B or C.

☆ Read the scale and move your counter on one place for each kilogram, for example for 3 kg move on 3 places.

☆ Read the new scale and keep moving in the same way.

☆ Which prize will you win for each starting position?

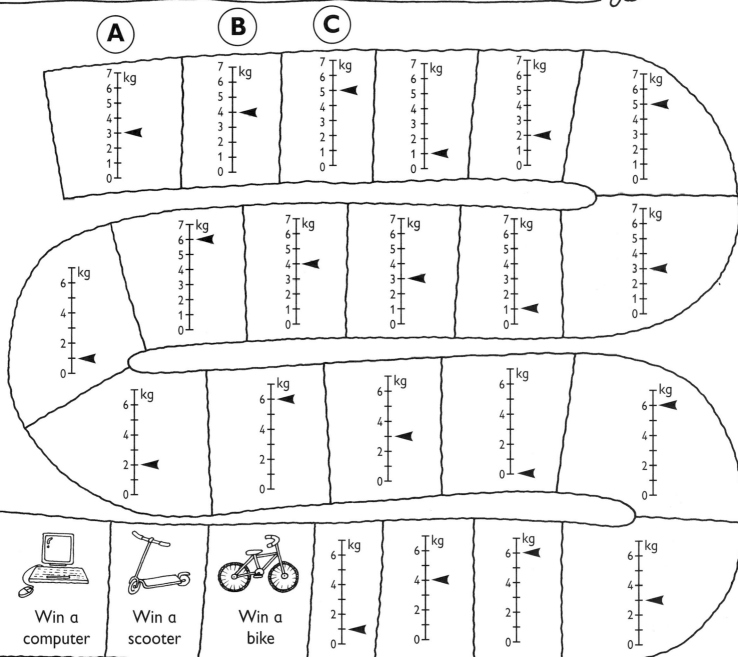

**Teachers' note** Note that the later scales are numbered in twos, with intermediate points unnumbered.

**100% New Developing Mathematics
Understanding Shapes and
Measures: Ages 6–7
© A & C BLACK**

# Monster weights

- ## Read the scales to find the weight of each monster.

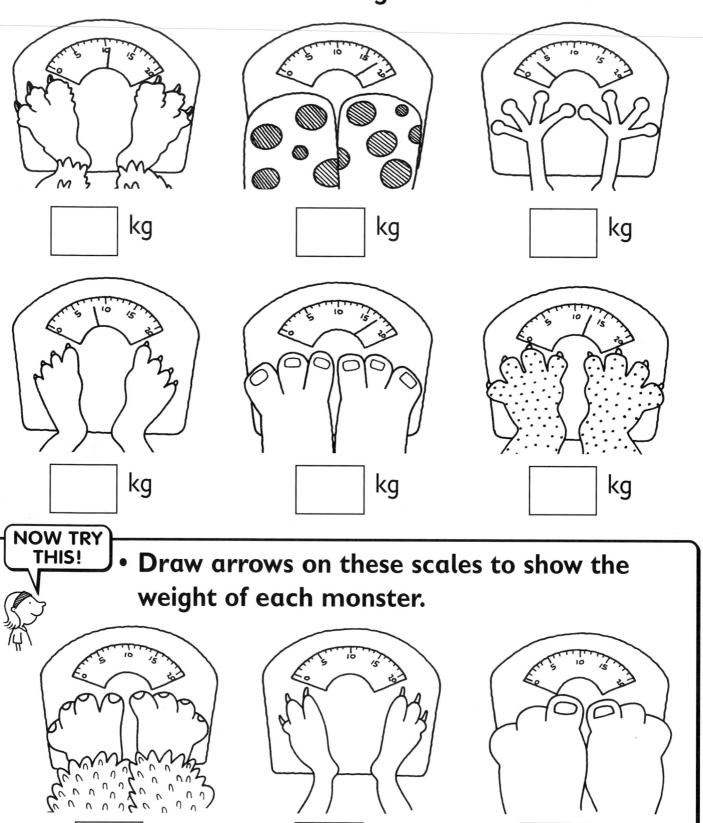

☐ kg   ☐ kg   ☐ kg

☐ kg   ☐ kg   ☐ kg

**NOW TRY THIS!**

- ## Draw arrows on these scales to show the weight of each monster.

| 14 | kg   | 4 | kg   | 19 | kg |

**Teachers' note** Ask the children to say which monster is the heaviest and which is the lightest. Encourage them to describe how they worked out how heavy each monster was using the scale. The arrows on the scales could be changed to create variety.

**100% New Developing Mathematics
Understanding Shapes and
Measures: Ages 6–7
© A & C BLACK**

# Deep water

- **Colour to show the correct amount of water in each bucket.**

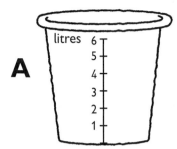

**A**

just over 1 litre

**B**

about 3 litres

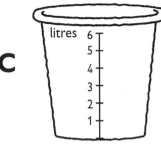

**C**

nearly 5 litres

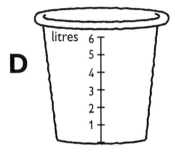

**D**

just less than 6 litres

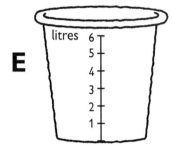

**E**

just under 4 litres

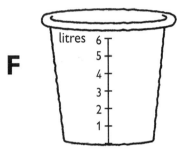

**F**

about half a litre

**G**

2 and a bit litres

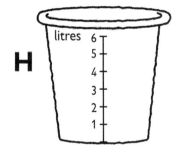

**H**

about 6 litres

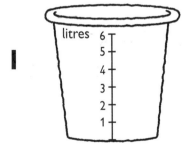

**I**

just over 3 litres

**NOW TRY THIS!**

- **Which bucket is holding the most water?** _____
- **Which bucket is holding the least water?** _____

**Teachers' note** Ensure that the children are introduced to 1-litre containers and that they begin to appreciate their size. Support this activity with practical measuring using sand or water containers.

**100% New Developing Mathematics
Understanding Shapes and
Measures: Ages 6–7**
© A & C BLACK

# Dizzy the baker: 1

Dizzy baked some cakes. Each cake needed a different length of time in the oven.

- Join each cake with the timer set to the correct length of time.

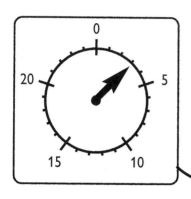  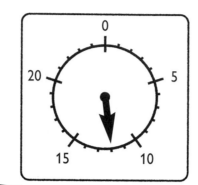  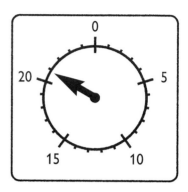

 **8 minutes**    **19 minutes**   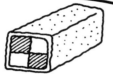 **12 minutes**    **3 minutes**    **23 minutes**    **21 minutes**

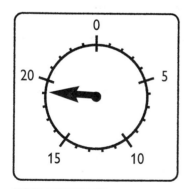  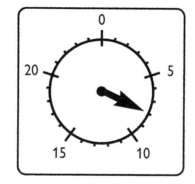  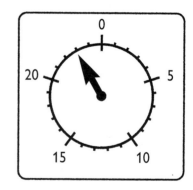

**NOW TRY THIS!**

- Draw an arrow on each dial to show these times.

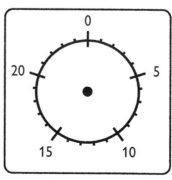

**13 minutes**   **24 minutes**

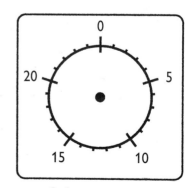

**Teachers' note** Draw children's attention to the fact that the timer shows up to 25 minutes only. The following sheet can be used as an extension activity as the timer shows up to one hour.

**100% New Developing Mathematics Understanding Shapes and Measures: Ages 6–7**
© A & C BLACK

# Dizzy the baker: 2

Dizzy baked some cakes. Each cake needed
a different length of time in the oven.

- **Join each cake with the timer set to
the correct length of time.**

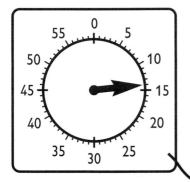 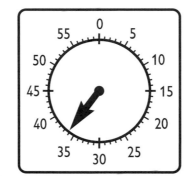 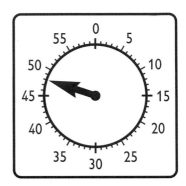

**29 minutes**

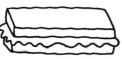
**23 minutes**

**14 minutes**

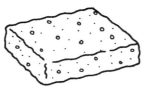
**48 minutes**

**36 minutes**

**59 minutes**

 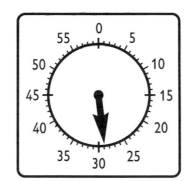 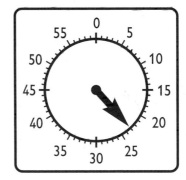

**NOW TRY THIS!**

- **Draw an
arrow on
each dial
to show
these times.**

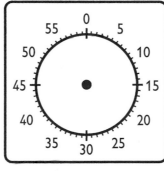
**44 minutes**

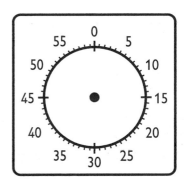
**58 minutes**

**Teachers' note** Watch out for children who make errors such as thinking that the position to the
right of 30 is 31 rather than 29. Draw attention to the multiples of 5 and ask which two of them
29 lies between.

**100% New Developing Mathematics
Understanding Shapes and
Measures: Ages 6–7**
© A & C BLACK

# Flea party

- **Draw lines with a ruler to join pairs of fleas together.**
- **Measure each line to the nearest centimetre and complete the sentences.**

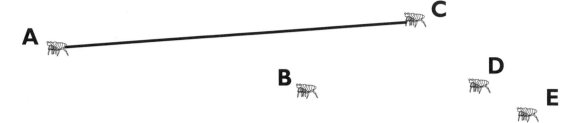

**A** **C**

**B** **D**

**E**

**F**

**G**

1. Flea __A__ is | 9 | cm from flea __C__ .

2. Flea ____ is |   | cm from flea ____ .

3. Flea ____ is |   | cm from flea ____ .

4. Flea ____ is |   | cm from flea ____ .

5. Flea ____ is |   | cm from flea ____ .

6. Flea ____ is |   | cm from flea ____ .

7. Flea ____ is |   | cm from flea ____ .

**NOW TRY THIS!**

- **Which 2 fleas are closest together?** _____
- **Which 2 are furthest apart?** _____

Teachers' note Ensure that children understand that they can join any two fleas and measure the distance between them with a ruler. Demonstrate how to hold the ruler and to place it so that the cm or zero mark is at the first flea. They should then read where the second flea is. Encourage them to turn the paper as appropriate.

100% New Developing Mathematic
Understanding Shapes and
Measures: Ages 6–7
© A & C BLACK

# Spaghetti spikes

- **Use a ruler to measure the lengths of uncooked spaghetti in centimetres.**

_Spaghetti_

☐ cm

☐ cm

☐ cm

☐ cm

☐ cm

**NOW TRY THIS!**

- **Use some string to measure the lengths of these pieces of cooked spaghetti.**

☐ cm

☐ cm

☐ cm

**Teachers' note** For the extension activity demonstrate how to place string along the line and then mark the string at the end before placing along a ruler, pulled tight. Children can then work in pairs when measuring with string. Discuss the children's answers to see who was most accurate.

*100% New Developing Mathematics* **Understanding Shapes and Measures: Ages 6–7** © A & C BLACK

# Frog tongues!

These frogs have long tongues for catching flies.
The length of each tongue is given in centimetres.

- Use a ruler to draw each tongue to see if the frog
  will reach the fly.

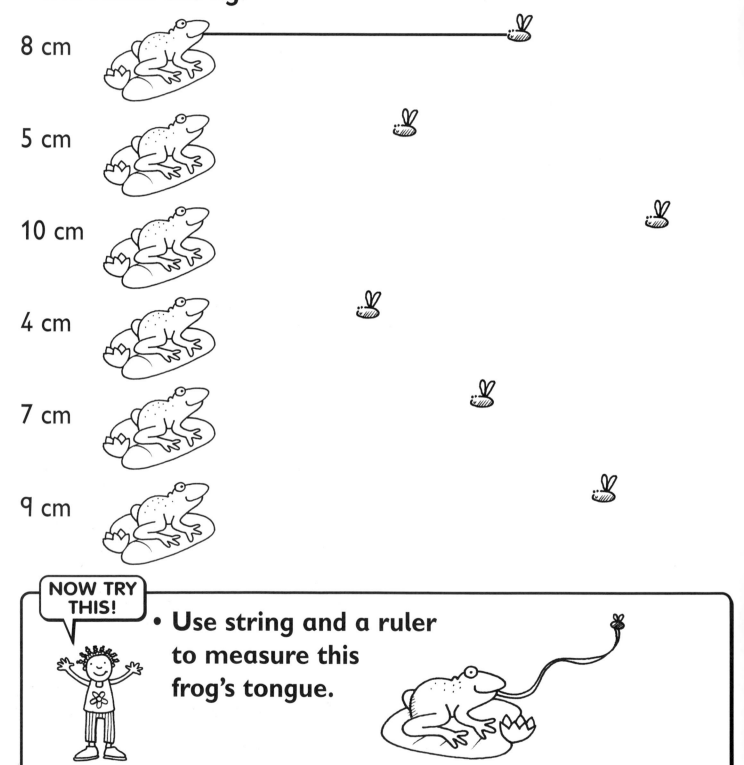

8 cm

5 cm

10 cm

4 cm

7 cm

9 cm

**NOW TRY THIS!**

- Use string and a ruler
  to measure this
  frog's tongue.

Teachers' note Ensure that children are not given rules (where the end of the rule is zero) but are given rulers (where the zero position is a little way along the ruler). Remind them to position the cm or zero mark on the ruler at each frog's mouth and to make a mark at the number of centimetres given, before joining the two.

100% New Developing Mathemati
Understanding Shapes and
Measures: Ages 6–7
© A & C BLACK

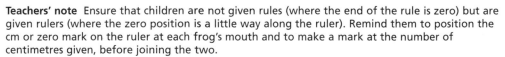

# Ant trail

An ant is walking all the way around the sides of each shape.

- Use a ruler to measure how far it walks for each shape.

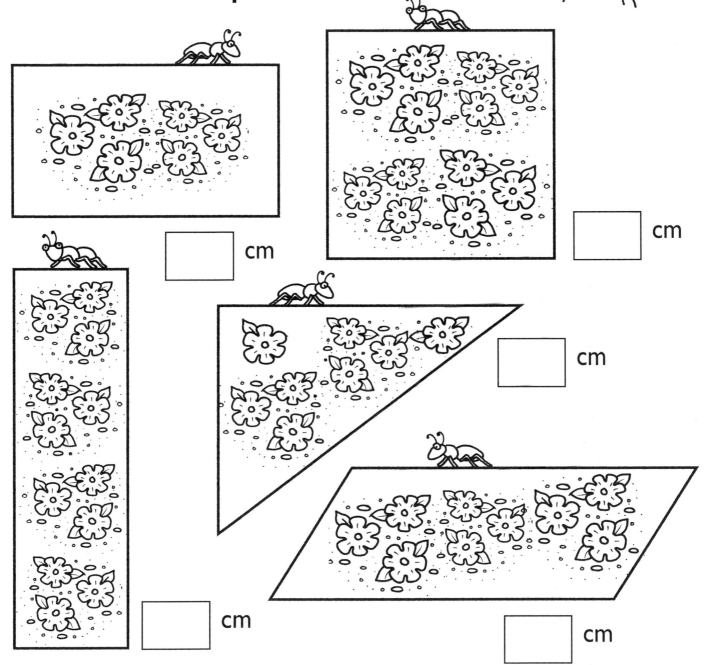

cm

cm

cm

cm

cm

**NOW TRY THIS!**

- **On the back of the sheet draw a rectangle that has an ant trail of 30 cm.**

**Teachers' note** Encourage the children to write the length of each side on the shape and then to find the total of the four lengths at the end. This can help them to further appreciate that opposite sides of rectangles are the same length and that only two sides of rectangles need to be measured.

*100% New Developing Mathematics*
**Understanding Shapes and**
**Measures: Ages 6–7**
© A & C BLACK

**55**

# Fun time

Alfie was taken to the theme park.

- **Fill in the missing unit of time in each box.**
- **Choose from:** [ seconds ] [ minutes ] [ hours ]

**1.** We took the train to the theme park. It took about 1 [ hour ] .

**2.** We had to queue for tickets. That took about 5 [        ] .

**3.** I went on the Big Wheel. I was on there for about 10 [        ] .

**4.** I fed a carrot to a horse. It ate it in about 20 [        ] .

**5.** We had fish and chips for lunch. That took about 15 [        ] .

**6.** We went on a boat trip for about 20 [        ] .

**7.** Then I ate an ice cream. That took about 8 [        ] .

**8.** We were at the theme park for about 5 [        ] altogether.

**NOW TRY THIS!**

- **Write some things you do that take:**

  10 minutes _____

  5 seconds _____

  8 hours _____

**Teachers' note** At the start of the lesson describe a visit to a theme park such as Alfie's day and discuss how we can describe how long things take. Ask the children to say which takes longer, a minute, an hour or a second, and invite them to say how long they think activities usually take, for example eating breakfast, doing the register, sitting in assembly.

100% New Developing Mathematics
Understanding Shapes and
Measures: Ages 6–7
© A & C BLACK

# Charlie and Chester

The chimps, Charlie and Chester, take different lengths of time to do the same thing.

- Tick who takes ⬚ longer ⬚ each time.

| | | Charlie | Chester |
|---|---|---|---|
| **1.** | swinging in the trees | ☐ 20 seconds | ✔ 1 minute |
| **2.** | hunting for food | ☐ 1 hour | ☐ 40 minutes |
| **3.** | playing | ☐ 30 minutes | ☐ 1 hour |
| **4.** | sleeping | ☐ 1 hour | ☐ 65 minutes |
| **5.** | making a nest | ☐ 6 minutes | ☐ 5 minutes |
| **6.** | eating a banana | ☐ 1 minute | ☐ 50 seconds |
| **7.** | sheltering from the rain | ☐ 1 day | ☐ 25 hours |

**NOW TRY THIS!**

- **Who takes longer?**

| | Charlie | Chester |
|---|---|---|
| Peeling fruit | ☐ 2 minutes | ☐ 100 seconds |

**Teachers' note** At the start of the lesson, discuss the relationships between the units of time: seconds, minutes, hours and days and write the relationships on the board, for example 60 seconds is the same as 1 minute. As a further extension activity, the children could work in pairs to time each other doing a simple activity to see who takes the longest.

**100% New Developing Mathematics Understanding Shapes and Measures: Ages 6–7 © A & C BLACK**

# Wally's wonder watch: 1

• **Draw hands on Wally's watch to match the times.**

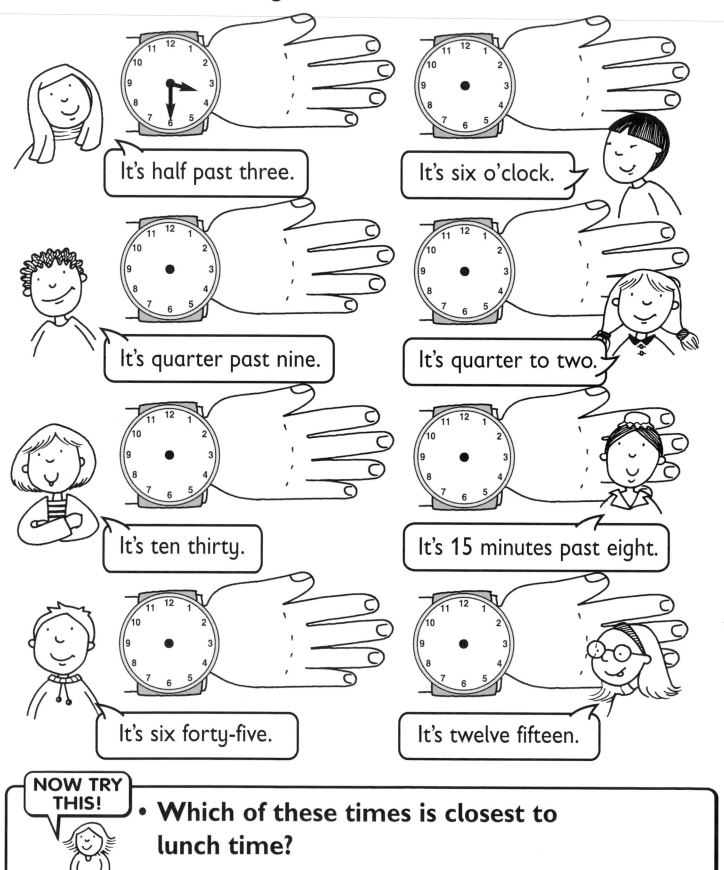

It's half past three.

It's six o'clock.

It's quarter past nine.

It's quarter to two.

It's ten thirty.

It's 15 minutes past eight.

It's six forty-five.

It's twelve fifteen.

**NOW TRY THIS!**

• **Which of these times is closest to lunch time?**

**Teachers' note** This activity can be used as an assessment to see which forms of describing times children are comfortable with, for example many will know quarter and half past but may be less familiar with six fifteen and seven forty-five. Draw attention to the fact that the hour hand points directly to the hour only at 'o'clock'.

**100% New Developing Mathematics
Understanding Shapes and
Measures: Ages 6–7**
© A & C BLACK

# Wally's wonder watch: 2

• **Write the times shown on Wally's watch in words.**

It's five o'clock.

It's

It's

It's

It's

It's

It's

It's

**NOW TRY THIS!**

• **Write the times on the last 4 watches in a different way.**

**Teachers' note** This activity can be used as an assessment to see how confident the children are in describing time in words. Note that there are several ways of describing time, for example six fifteen, quarter past six, 15 minutes past six, or half nine, half past nine, nine thirty, 30 minutes past nine.

**100% New Developing Mathematics**
**Understanding Shapes and**
**Measures: Ages 6–7**
© A & C BLACK

# Carol's classy clock: 1

- **Write the digital time on Carol's clock to match the times.**

**8:00**

It's eight o'clock.

**:**

It's ten thirty.

**:**

It's two fifteen.

**:**

It's nine forty-five.

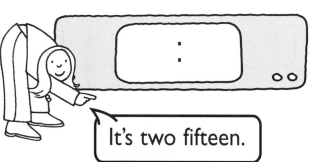

**:**

It's half past eleven.

**:**

It's 15 minutes past one.

**:**

It's quarter past three.

**:**

It's quarter to twelve.

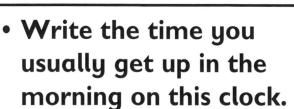

**NOW TRY THIS!**

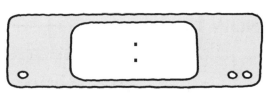

- **Write the time you usually get up in the morning on this clock.**

**:**

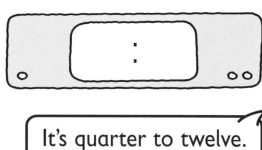

---

**Teachers' note** This activity can be used as an assessment to see which forms of describing digital times children are comfortable with, for example many will find writing times such as six fifteen and seven forty-five in digital form much easier than writing half past seven or quarter to nine.

**100% New Developing Mathematics Understanding Shapes and Measures: Ages 6–7 © A & C BLACK**

- **Write the times on Carol's clock in words. Use words from this list:**

| o'clock | quarter past | half past | quarter to |
|---|---|---|---|

5:30 — It's half past five.

11:00 — It's

7:15 — It's

8:45 — It's

9:00 — It's

6:15 — It's

12:30 — It's

4:45 — It's

**NOW TRY THIS!**

- **Which of the times above is closest to 5 o'clock?** _____

**Teachers' note** This activity can be used as an assessment to see whether the children are confident in relating the times shown on digital clock with half past, quarter past, quarter to, etc. Remind children that the hour comes first when shown on a digital clock and draw attention to the fact that for times with :45, it is the next hour that is written, for example 2:45 is quarter to three.

**100% New Developing Mathematics
Understanding Shapes and
Measures: Ages 6–7**
© A & C BLACK

# TV times: 1

| The time now is | Cartoons are at |
|---|---|
|  |  |

| The time now is | The Y factor is at |
|---|---|
|  |  |

| The time now is | The news is at |
|---|---|
|  |  |

| The time now is | Football is at |
|---|---|
|  |  |

| The time now is | Art-magic is at |
|---|---|
|  |  |

| The time now is | Em street is at |
|---|---|
|  |  |

| The time now is | Nowastory is at |
|---|---|
|  |  |

| The time now is | Dinoworld is at |
|---|---|
|  |  |

| The time now is | Dina Warrior is at |
|---|---|
|  |  |

| The time now is | Westenders is at |
|---|---|
|  |  |

**Teachers' note** This sheet should be used in conjunction with page 63. It could also be used alone by asking the children to write down how long they would have to wait for each programme.

**100% New Developing Mathematics
Understanding Shapes and
Measures: Ages 6–7**
© A & C BLACK

I must wait for **30** minutes.

I must wait for **half an hour**.

I must wait for **45** minutes.

I must wait for **15** minutes.

I must wait for **1 hour**.

I must wait for **quarter of an hour**.

I must wait for **60** minutes.

I must wait for **three quarters of an hour**.

I must wait for **2 hours**.

I must wait for **1 hour**.

**Teachers' note** Ask the children to cut out the cards from TV times: 1 and 2 and sort them into pairs. The sheet could also be used alone. Children could be given a time and told to find what time each programme would start. Both sets of cards could also be used by children working in pairs, such as by turning over a card of each type and seeing whether they match.

**100% New Developing Mathematics
Understanding Shapes and
Measures: Ages 6–7
© A & C BLACK**

# Time quiz

- **Help the team answer the questions.**
- **Circle the correct answer.**

**1.** It is 8:00. What time will it be in half an hour?

| | | | |
|---|---|---|---|
| **a** | 7:30 | **b** | 8:00 |
| **c** | 8:30 | **d** | 8:15 |

**2.** It is 5:30. What time was it 30 minutes ago?

| | | | |
|---|---|---|---|
| **a** | 6:30 | **b** | 6:00 |
| **c** | 5:15 | **d** | 5:00 |

**3.** It is 3:00. What time will it be in 15 minutes?

| | | | |
|---|---|---|---|
| **a** | 3:30 | **b** | 2:45 |
| **c** | 3:15 | **d** | 2:30 |

**4.** It is 1:15. What time was it 45 minutes ago?

| | | | |
|---|---|---|---|
| **a** | 12:45 | **b** | 12:15 |
| **c** | 12:30 | **d** | 1:30 |

**5.** It is 10:00. What time was it half an hour ago?

| | | | |
|---|---|---|---|
| **a** | 10:30 | **b** | 9:00 |
| **c** | 9:30 | **d** | 11:15 |

**6.** It is 6:45. What time was it 15 minutes ago?

| | | | |
|---|---|---|---|
| **a** | 7:00 | **b** | 6:15 |
| **c** | 7:30 | **d** | 6:30 |

**7.** It is 4:45. What time will it be in three quarters of an hour?

| | | | |
|---|---|---|---|
| **a** | 6:30 | **b** | 4:30 |
| **c** | 5:30 | **d** | 6:00 |

**8.** It is 7:30. What time will it be in quarter of an hour?

| | | | |
|---|---|---|---|
| **a** | 7:15 | **b** | 7:45 |
| **c** | 8:00 | **d** | 8:15 |

**NOW TRY THIS!**

- **Make up four more questions for a partner to solve.**

Teachers' note The times can be altered before copying to provide more challenging questions, such as involving time to the nearest 5-minute intervals rather than to quarters of a hour. Point out that some questions involve moving forwards and others moving backwards in time.

100% New Developing Mathematics
Understanding Shapes and
Measures: Ages 6–7
© A & C BLACK